PAJ Books
Bonnie Marranca and Gautam Dasgupta
Series Editors

Art + Performance
Meredith Monk, edited by Deborah Jowitt
Rachel Rosenthal, edited by Moira Roth
Reza Abdoh, edited by Daniel Mufson
Richard Foreman, edited by Gerald Rabkin

Reza Abdoh

Edited by Daniel Mufson

A PAJ Book

The Johns Hopkins University Press   Baltimore + London

© 1999 The Johns Hopkins University Press
All rights reserved. Published 1999
Printed in the United States of America on acid-free paper

9 8 7 6 5 4 3 2 1

The Johns Hopkins University Press
2715 North Charles Street
Baltimore, Maryland 21218-4363
www.press.jhu.edu

Library of Congress Cataloging-in-Publication Data will be
found at the end of this book.

A catalog record for this book is available from the British Library.

ISBN 0-8018-6123-3
ISBN 0-8018-6124-1 (pbk.)

Frontispiece. Left to right: Juliana Francis, Tom Fitzpatrick,
Gerard Little, Tom Pearl, Reza Abdoh, Rafael Pimental.
Photo: Annie Leibovitz.

In memory of my parents, Ann and Marvin Mufson, and of Reza Abdoh

Schließlich brauchen sie uns nicht mehr, die
  Früheentrückten,
man entwöhnt sich des Irdischen sanft , wie man
  den Brüsten
milde der Mutter entwächst. Aber wir, die so große
Geheimnisse brauchen, denen aus Trauer so oft
seliger Fortschritt entspringt—: *könnten* wir sein
  ohne sie?

In the end they need us no longer, they who died
  young;
one stops thirsting for what is earthly the way a
  child
outgrows its mother's breast. But we,
who need such great mysteries, for whom blessed
  progress
springs from grief—: *could* we exist without them?

—Rilke, *Duineser Elegien (Duino Elegies)*

Contents

Photograph gallery follows page 88.

Acknowledgments

Many thanks to Bonnie Marranca for her advice regarding the content and structure of this anthology; to Linda Tripp and Anne Whitmore at the Johns Hopkins University Press, for their patience and advice; and to James Leverett, Gordon Rogoff, Elinor Fuchs, Joe Martin Hill, and Anna Beth Martin for their numerous, helpful criticisms of my introductory essay. Various members of Reza Abdoh's company, Dar A Luz, have been supportive and helpful: above all, producer Diane White, but also Adam Soch, Brendan Doyle, Juliana Francis, and Adam Leipzig. My thanks also to my family, who have always given me their utmost support and most honest criticism, and to Mirjam Honisch, who provided motivation when my own flagged. I would also like to thank all of the contributors to the anthology, most of whom participated in this project without receiving any remuneration save the satisfaction of contributing to the discourse on Abdoh's work. And thanks, of course, to Greg Gunter, who in 1994 took me to see a play, *Quotations from a Ruined City,* by a person whose work neither of us knew, Reza Abdoh.

Reza Abdoh

Daniel Mufson

Introduction:

The Sickness Proper to the Time

By the time he died of AIDS in the spring of 1995 at age 32, Reza Abdoh had written, assembled, and directed well over a dozen works for the stage, creating a great stir in that small community of artists, academics, and critics who concern themselves with alternative theater. Born in Iran, Abdoh spent most of his youth in London or Los Angeles, and his works, though international in scope, felt distinctly American, drenched as they were in influences from American popular culture. The structure of the works themselves hinted at the intense mélange, the chaotic heterogeneity, that has come to be most strongly associated with the American city, especially with the dynamism of those cities where his work was performed—L.A. and, later, New York. By the time his idiosyncratic and vigorous company, Dar A Luz, lined up for its curtain call, one felt as exhausted as the cast should have looked. Abdoh's works, American in their brashness, iconoclasm, and endless playfulness, were nonetheless atypical of American theater, above all in their vehement rejection of sentimentality, happy endings, and a world in which moral ambiguity is swept aside for the clearly defined realms of Good and Evil, Victim and Victimizer. Abdoh knew he was infected with HIV well before he was 25 years old, and that awareness fueled in his work an urgency to which smallness of thought and gesture was anathema.

Abdoh filled his works with tension: tension born of moral and formal contradictions; tension born of tone oscillating wildly from frenzy to calm; tension born of the negotiation between poetic and profane, traditional and modern, normal and abnormal. Apropos of all of Abdoh's work is the dialectic described by Theodor Adorno in *Minima Moralia,* where he defines the "sickness proper to the time" as in fact being "normality." To describe the pernicious facade of health used to

1

conceal evidence of a diseased "psychic economy," Adorno cites the verses "Wretchedness remains. When all is said, / It cannot be uprooted, live or dead. / So it is made invisible instead." Abdoh's productions seem to flow from an implicit recognition of Adorno's critique, and they in turn consistently endeavor to locate the wretched in the normal and vice versa. One of the surprising aspects of Abdoh's work was that it was able to render wretchedness shocking to a society that ordinarily considers itself numbed to depictions of its own dejectedness.

Less often discussed but perhaps all the more remarkable, however, is the degree to which Abdoh's attack on the sickness of the "psychic economy" was characterized by a distinctively ecstatic energy and incisive wit. The multitude of his aims and his determination to achieve them were, in fact, wonderfully uneconomical; a playwright and director of calculated excess, Abdoh strove to jolt people out of complacency, to uncover hidden malignancies in the culture, to create a poetically ambiguous vocabulary of images and text, to lace his portraits with humor, and, finally, "to create a work that is entrancing," as he told me in his last interview. Even had he not accomplished as many of his aims to the extent that he did, he would have been notable for the unusual breadth and quality of his ambitions alone.

The only primary text in this anthology, the script for Abdoh's *The Hip-Hop Waltz of Eurydice*, exemplifies stylistic attributes that characterize all of his plays. A brief analysis of it should provide as good an introduction as any to Abdoh's art. *Hip-Hop* displaces the myth of Orpheus and Eurydice to an imaginary realm that exists out of time: Orpheus types on a typewriter and listens to a 1940s-style radio as the sink drips incessantly, Eurydice urinates into a bucket and uses a hair dryer to dry herself. Abdoh transforms the myth into a story of sexual repression, where Eurydice is seized and taken to the underworld as punishment for her lustful desires. He peppers his adaptation with allusions to St. George's dragon-slaying, Rilke, and Cocteau, while large swaths of dialogue are modified excerpts from the Dolly Parton movie *9 to 5* and the radio series *The Bickersons*. In his very use of *9 to 5* and *The Bickersons*, Abdoh was following the lead set by Cocteau in his 1950 film, *Orphée*, in which Orpheus and Eurydice are demoted to the level of Parisian bourgeois. Abdoh takes the couple down one notch lower by occasionally making them speak in the vocabulary of the American sit-com. By recontextualizing dialogue from *The Bickersons* and *9 to 5*, Abdoh creates several scenes in *Hip-Hop* that are simultaneously amusing and discomforting, as, for example, when *9 to 5*'s lighthearted rendition of sexual harassment in the workplace—used twice in *Hip-Hop*, the second time with the genders reversed—quickly gives way to brutality.

Although Abdoh himself has described *Hip-Hop* as a parable of the repression of homosexuality, its moral universe does not conjure a simple struggle between good and evil forces. When we first hear the voice of authority as embodied by "the Captain," the actor who portrays him, Alan Mandell, is still offstage. "Eros," says the deep, disembodied voice, came "from the egg laid by night. . . . We will cure you of your perversions." This first auditory impression of a purely repressive figure is soon undermined when the Captain finally emerges to seize Eurydice. Obese, covered with warts, sauntering with a sensual arrogance, the Captain reveals himself as Satan ascendant, a sadistic glutton determined to forbid anyone else the very indulgences he most avidly seeks. Indeed, the act of prohibition itself provides a decadent joy for the Captain, who tosses Orpheus on a bed and with an ominous growl vows to "bore desire right out of you"—invoking an image of penetration in the promise to deny penetration.

The two most memorable sections of the performance, however, come in the Captain's monologues that open and close the last section of the play, titled "Alan's Final Solution." What I am here calling the Captain's first monologue begins "One God. One Party," and ends with the repeated question, "Is my body now obsolete?" The speech is interrupted in the script, but in performance the interjections from Orpheus and Eurydice lend orchestral support to what is clearly the Captain's aria—the interjections provide ballast and stimulus for a long and powerful speech that laces wide-ranging images and narratives into a surprisingly unified whole. Somehow, Abdoh preserves all of the Captain's repugnant qualities while endowing him with a tragic solitude and an eternal sense of unfulfilled desires. The Captain's monologue, an assault as much against himself as against the audience, takes place on several levels. The opening question, about a shave and a haircut, is the first in an intermittent string of worries about physical appearance; the second question, about divine influence, commences a rhetorical mocking of self-seriousness—physical vanity on the one hand and the vanity of "accomplishments" on the other. "I am obsessed with the little toe on my left foot," the Captain explains. "It is turning into a claw. A species that is going nowhere. And I'm having to do this alone. Not like Cousteau with his assiduous team aboard the sun-flooded schooner but here. Alone. Alone. Alone." The speech articulates the Captain's confident dismissal of earnest endeavor. "Busy young creatures, you don't have a chance," the Captain laughs, after having had an audience member read aloud a card saying "I'm a self starter. I enjoy and am excited by producing." At the same time, though, the speech slowly reveals—to the audience and to the Captain himself—the hollowness of the Captain's dissolute pleasures. Mixed in with a series of trivial questions and answers on topics ranging from Oprah Winfrey to opportunity cost, and interrupted by occasional moralizing about social etiquette, a detailed narrative describes a tawdry bar scene with an Asian catamite. Eruptions of fear at the thought of aging and death, scattered throughout the script, reach their saturation point here. The result provokes a peculiar mixture of revulsion and sympathy.

These speeches nullify any equations or glosses that would define Orpheus and Eurydice as the homosexual couple and the Captain as the force of heterosexual oppression. "I want to taste every man and every girl," the Captain says in the first of the two monologues. More dramatically, it is the Captain who ends the play by intruding, emaciated and shivering as if terminally ill, upon the suburban utopia of Orpheus and Eurydice. "I know I have loved too much. I have stuffed too many bodies, used up too many orange skies. I ought to be stamped out," he says, and the lights fade to darkness as the audience hears only the Captain's erratic breathing and the howling of wolves. A disquieting close, it inverts the hierarchy of power and sympathy established early on, and it is hard not to hear a little of Abdoh himself in the Captain's lines in this, the first script Abdoh wrote after learning he was infected with HIV.

The writing style of the Captain's first speech also shows off Abdoh's playwriting at its height. Abdoh, influenced by the "cut-up technique" as used by William S. Burroughs in *The Third Mind,* uses a great deal of found materials in his works (especially in *Tight Right White*), and, in his arrangement and staging of these quotations, he demonstrates prowess mainly as *bricoleur* and director. But when he writes his own material well, he achieves a different kind of virtuosity in a style simultaneously desultory and focused. Abdoh pursues the juxtaposition of extremes with unwavering fanaticism. "Anyone want a shave and a haircut?" the Captain asks the audience with an earnestness that belies the apparent absurdity of the question; then, coming down off the stage to address the audience from the house, he asks in the same tone, "You! Do you believe God will touch you?" Abdoh exploits such contrasts to amuse his spectators as often as he does to disturb them.

In this respect, the style of the Captain's speech characterizes the task and art of all of Abdoh's later works: by indirections to find directions out. One sees this throughout *Quotations from a Ruined City*, the last work Abdoh produced, which among other things bonded the language of entrepreneurship to narratives of Serbian war crimes. *Tight Right White* was a hybrid of a blaxploitation movie and, as he put it, a Borscht Belt vaudeville routine. *The Law of Remains* brings Jeffrey Dahmer into confrontation with Andy Warhol, Ronald Reagan, and God as embodied by a Puerto Rican transvestite named Lola Beltran. *Bogeyman*, perhaps his most autobiographical piece, mixes images of the BDSM (bondage-domination, sado-masochism) scene with midwestern prairie landscapes and mingles a mother dressed as the bride of Frankenstein with repeated references to one of the most sympathetic of maternal figures in the Old Testament, Rachel. Abdoh's work—both the texts and the images created by the stagings—cohere by virtue of their contrasts.

Several critics perceive the distanced style of performance adopted by the actors and the political commitment of the *oeuvre* as being in kinship with Brecht. An equally important bond between Abdoh and Brecht would be the use of what critic Franco Ruffini, writing in the *New Theatre Quarterly*, calls vertical montage, or the Bruegel effect.[1] As Bruegel the Elder does most famously in *The Fall of Icarus*, Abdoh relentlessly splits the focus between scenes and actions that remain separated spatially yet comment upon one another in their simultaneity. Abdoh uses this technique at least as early as his 1986 production *A Medea: Requiem for a Boy with a White White Toy*, where the stage was a high school gymnasium viewed lengthwise. In his *Los Angeles Times* review of *A Medea* (not reprinted here), Robert Koehler praises this "depth of field perspective" which "makes your head feel like a camera focusing, panning and tracking across an increasingly wondrous landscape." Abdoh's use of vertical montage reaches its frenzied height in *Bogeyman*, in which the stage is divided into at least ten, perhaps eleven, distinct playing areas where diverse actions often occur simultaneously in two, three, or more sections.

If no individual aspect of Abdoh's work is unique, the way he assembles all he borrows does indeed amount to something that theater had not seen before. As John Bell persuasively argues, Abdoh borrows aspects of other artists' vocabularies, from Brecht to Richard Foreman, to create his own language. He pays homage to tools of the avant-garde that have become—in spite of themselves—conventions, but at the same time adds his own unmistakable style to what can now be recognized as the oxymoron of an avant-garde heritage. His example will be of use to playwrights and to *auteur* directors who, like Foreman, Robert Wilson in his early work, and Anne Bogart with her "Theater Essays," link a philosophy of staging visual images to playwriting models that have to be invented as needed, in defiance of tradition, creating their own genre. Abdoh, more brazenly than the other artists mentioned, uses tradition to alter tradition.

Fortunately, Abdoh leaves behind an extensive record of his work on video. Archives are being established on the east and west coasts of the United States and in Minneapolis. In California, the videos will be available at Cal Arts; in Minneapolis, at the Walker Arts Center. In New York, the Library for the Performing Arts at Lincoln Center will house not only the video collection, but also articles, programs, and Abdoh's correspondence. The quality of the tapes varies, but the smaller scale of *Hip-Hop Waltz* and *Quotations* and their use of a proscenium stage facilitated a better video representation of them than of the other performances. While no one will argue that video can capture the experience of seeing a work in the theater, those with a bit of imagination should be able to make great use of the tapes, especially when viewing them is coupled with an examination of the playscripts themselves and reviewers' vivid descriptions. Such resources are not to be underestimated. Even the primitive, silent 8 mm recordings made by the German filmmaker Syberberg of Brecht's *Herr Puntila, Die Mutter,* and *Urfaust* (all 1953) are of tremendous value for learning about Brecht's staging practices. The videos of Abdoh's stage works, filmed and edited by Adam Soch, who was also responsible for the videos that Abdoh incorporated into his productions, are of remarkably high quality given the paucity of resources for such endeavors.

Although relatively little has been written about Abdoh, enough material exists to have made the process of deciding what to include more than difficult. I have not included reviews of anything prior to *Minamata,* for two reasons: first, all of the productions discussed here are recorded on video of fairly good quality, which is not true of all of the earlier work; and second, while Abdoh directed many plays prior to *Minamata* that he did not write or that he co-wrote, most of the works done afterwards—after he found out he was infected with HIV—were products of his vision alone: his writing, his *mise en scène.*

I selected the reviews and essays based on the vividness of their description, the quality of analysis, and, as much as possible, the diversity of analysis. There are two results. First, *Father Was a Peculiar Man* goes undiscussed, as none of the reviews, including the positive ones, manages to describe the site-specific performance with much detail or to explain its connection to Dostoyevsky's *The Brothers Karamazov,* upon which the script is based. Second, a common type of review goes unrepresented, the one in which a critic reacts solely with shock and indignation to the violence and obscenity of the language and images. In a typical review of *Law of Remains, Newsday's* Julius Novick wrote, "It's nauseating, all right, but is it art?" Too often, such comments constitute nothing more than rhetorical posturing when they might otherwise have provided an opportunity for a more intense critical reflection. Instead, I have included examples of the more intriguing and not altogether uncommon type of response evoked by Abdoh's performances, from the early ones in L.A. days to the final ones in New York: a critic concedes that Abdoh possesses a certain genius and then struggles to explain why he or she dislikes or even abhors the production at hand. Part of the appeal of Michael Feingold's review of *Tight Right White* is the sincerity and visceral nature of his response, acknowledging Abdoh's brilliance while examining his own revulsion for the play and questioning its ethical underpinnings. Charles Marowitz, too, sounds equivocal in describing *Bogeyman,* a work that clearly captivated and impressed him but that ultimately struck him as "one-sided" and "too engrossed in condemning evil to work out a strategy to combat it." Similarly, Stephen Holden notes Abdoh's directorial skill but holds that "*The Law of Remains* continually undermines its own political ambitions" because the "sheer density of the noise and tumult make it hard to follow."

Sylvie Drake, one of the first critics to champion Abdoh, concedes in her review of *Minamata* that she needed to see the show twice in order to begin to appreciate it, and both of her reviews published here illustrate well the way in which a critic can wrestle with the new and develop a deep appreciation for an innovative talent. Elinor Fuchs, Gautam Dasgupta, Philippa Wehle, Marvin Carlson, and John Bell delve more deeply into the construction of the works and consider their resonance in terms both personal and historical. Wehle and Carlson round out Feingold's response to *Tight Right White* and approach the work in complementary ways: Wehle attempts a closer reading of the performance itself and the stimuli that created it, while Carlson relates *Tight Right White* to Abdoh's earlier works and defines his uniqueness among HIV-infected performance artists. Bell considers Abdoh as an artist bringing the avant-garde back to the realm of the political after a decade or more of formalist retreat. Bell also begins to probe the Iranian influences in Abdoh's work—an influence far from self-evident— and, perhaps most important, considers Abdoh's works in light of the theoretical ramifications of creating an avant-garde that is aware of and embraces its own traditions. Fuchs and Dasgupta approach the work on the most personal level, evoking broader aspects of Abdoh's vision throughout his *oeuvre*. Much has been omitted, and much remains to be said. Abdoh's 1992 film, *The Blind Owl,* has hardly been studied at all. With the printing of this anthology, the scripts for *Hip-Hop, The Law of Remains, Tight Right White,* and *Quotations from a Ruined City* have been published, but the densest text of all, *Bogeyman,* is not yet available. Nor is *Minamata.* As Abdoh considered himself a poet of the stage, so should he be treated, and many of the texts deserve close reading.

Although many critics discuss either Abdoh's shock tactics or the influence of Bataille, none has considered both together in any discussion of obscenity. In the days of the V-chip and the ever repeated mantra "family values," one is tempted to apologize for the obscenity of Abdoh's work or to cast it in a subordinate role. Obscenity is clearly vital to Abdoh's vision, but it is not merely a matter of tweaking Puritan sensibilities by injecting nudity, profanity, and violence into every production. Obscenity in Abdoh ties in with Bataille's description of the term as "our name for the uneasiness which upsets the physical state associated with self-possession, with the possession of a recognized and stable individuality."

For Bataille, sex compromises self-possession—it breaks down the facades that separate humanity from animality, autonomy from need. An erotic brand of obscenity exists in Abdoh's productions, where sexuality is so often harnessed to violence, a loss of dignity, and death. One also finds sociopolitical obscenity of the sort already pointed to in *Tight Right White,* where, as in *Peer Gynt,* we peel away the onion-like layers of identity to discover a simultaneously liberating and devastating emptiness. Even stage architecture—all encompassing as it is in *Tight Right White,* and to some extent in *The Law of Remains*—can threaten the audience's feeling of autonomy and self-possession, by making the spectators feel, as Michael Feingold felt, trapped in the confines of an alien imagination. *The Law of Remains* threatened the viewers' autonomy further by having an amplified Dominatrix-like voice bark out commands for the audience to move to new locations within the abandoned hotel where the show premiered in New York. Obscenity is the netherworld between separateness and connectedness. Obscenity finds itself between the intellect's striving for objectivity and the body's beholdenness to lust, decay, and death, a beholdenness that chains the individual to the species and its harsh history of endings and beginnings. Obscenity compromises humanity's vaunted position above the animal yet allows people to remain distant enough from the bestial to want to limit our identification with it. Bondage and domination, shaping the vision not only of *Law of Remains* but also of *Bogeyman,* fit naturally into a domain where humans willingly subject themselves to a wrathful master who doles out punishment for reward: often, we are complicit in our loss of dignity and control.

While the last few decades have had no paucity of racial and gender cross-casting, few have exploited the practice to such an extreme extent and with such varied results as Abdoh. The use of drag, heavy make-up, masks, and even masks over make-up constitutes a clear comment upon recent discussions about multicultural theory and identity politics, but the radical manipulation of appearance also draws on the traditions of satire. Abdoh takes demons quotidian and historical and caricatures them with a mix of mordant humor and earnest passion that at times recalls drawings and paintings by the likes of George Grosz and Otto Dix. In part, the resemblance is simply cosmetic, as the make-up caked on the Dar A Luz actors' faces often lends them a ghoulish air—the Captain's appearance in *Hip-Hop* could be the incarnation of any number of Grosz figures, from *Am Tisch* (1920–21) to the portrayal of Hindenburg in *Sonnenfinsternis* (1926). But Abdoh often paints caricatures in a way one might call exponential. The stereotypical Jew in *Tight Right White,* Moishe Pipik, is in this sense an exponential caricature: imagine one of the racist portraits of Jews propagated by *Der Stürmer,* and then imagine the caricature itself caricatured by someone like Grosz, and the final effect will be the one created by Pipik's character. *Tight Right White,* perhaps more than any of the other plays, lays bare the brutality intrinsic to the manufacturing of cultural identity by people within and outside ethnic groups. It lampoons the stereotypes that invariably constitute cultural identity, and yet, in the end, it suggests their inevitability and almost denies the possibility that one might be left with anything "authentic," even if stereotypes could be eradicated.

The satiric in Abdoh goes beyond the superficial level of distorting appearances; it underlies the spirit and motive behind most of the work's salient traits. Satirists exaggerate. They do not "do justice," as it were, to those they depict but distort the nature of their targets in order to reawaken disgust in an audience inured or blinded to qualities that have lost their "disturbational" (to use Arthur Danto's word) value. As a result, satire almost inevitably invites charges of obscenity and blasphemy. Satirists' art, then, contains inherent contradictions. On the one hand, their distorted representations of humanity tend to suggest a certain misanthropy, and yet satire strives to cause a reexamination and improvement in the lives of its audience—hardly a misanthropic goal. Furthermore, satirists leave themselves vulnerable to the criticism that they lack subtlety. They *do* lack subtlety, but they resort to extremes because they perceive the world around them as having blunted the collective sensibilities of their audience. The satirist magnifies a problem in order to allow it to be recognized. How, after all, could one possibly expect a song mourning subtlety's death to be itself subtle?

All of Abdoh's images—however gory, graphic, or pathetic they may be—spring from a deep humanism, the desire to teach people that, as Abdoh says in his interview with Howard Ross Patlis, "it's not enough to think of a world that is more livable. . . . you have to act on it." And here we come upon another apparent contradiction: on the one hand the desire to create work that is "entrancing," that eludes definition and does not compel any particular reaction from its audience, and on the other the desire to provoke the audience into examining itself and its surroundings and to take actions to improve both. As a result, Charles Marowitz, in his review of *Bogeyman,* can take Abdoh to task for being "too engrossed in condemning evil to work out a strategy to combat it," while the *New York Times* critic, Ben Brantley, can find the work "didactic," and still other critics can talk about the moral ambiguity of the work.

The urge to teach by instilling doubt and a courage to "say 'No' in thunder" has been a project of countless authors, a project too often ignored or misunderstood by critics. There are, I would argue, two tiers of so-called didactic literature: first, one in which artists present problems and/or solutions reductively, with a vehement advocacy for a position on an issue which, in itself, does not impinge on a broader philosophical outlook; and second, one in which artists try to teach by undermining confidence in a certain way of viewing the world and encouraging a reconsideration of values on a broad scale. Admittedly, the two will often overlap. Abdoh descends from time to time to the first, more provincial level, but overall his work belongs to the second.

In our Prozac-inflated era, in which art is so often forced to justify its existence by providing uplift or hope or redemption or compassion, Abdoh's vision cannot help but occupy a place in the margins, even being dismissed as an artifact of an aging avant-garde's morbid obsessions. The pathology of American culture becomes ever clearer: health, beauty, happiness, and wealth are ideals sought through denial of their opposites. Abdoh, perhaps because of his illness but more likely because of his intrinsically critical and analytical mind, evokes classical steeliness. Seneca, writing to Lucilius, discusses with admiration Epicurus's advice to "rehearse death." "You may possibly think it unnecessary to learn something which you will only have to put into practice once," Seneca writes. "That is the very reason we ought to be practicing it. We must needs continually study a thing if we are not in a position to test whether we know it." To Abdoh's credit, his plays never avert their gaze away from the abyss to which the playwright was prematurely destined, they almost never lapse into sentimentality, and they never indulge in self-pity.

Various critics, even sometimes Abdoh himself as critic of his own work, struggle to find redemption in these plays; I disagree with those who find it, but I would argue that the absence of redemption and convincing consolation constitutes an asset, not a fault. The stark resolution of Abdoh's works demonstrates a Socratic wisdom and courage; his rehearsals of death acknowledge and demonstrate that the greatest knowledge of death is a recognition that we know nothing about it, that we can do nothing to stop it, and that it is possible, in spite of fear, to embrace death as part of the natural course of existence. In this respect, Abdoh reveals the folly of the entire debate over whether or not art can be "therapeutic." A not-uncommon expression of the cultural argument that Abdoh's work helps to debunk can be found in *The Culture of Complaint,* by the art critic, Robert Hughes. "There is no generalizing about the moral effects of art," Hughes writes, "because it doesn't seem to have any. If it did, people who are constantly exposed to it, including all curators and critics, would be saints, and we are not." It is not even necessary to address the syllogism whereby Hughes implies that, because art does not necessitate reflection, art cannot aid reflection. More typical is the erroneous assumption that the examined life consists of some kind of twelve-step progress to ethical perfection or existential bliss. As Abdoh shows, the examined life—and, dialectically, the rehearsal of death—implies an undermining of exactly that form of moral and spiritual certainty. Abdoh's works, at their best, become didactic only by teaching an anti-knowledge, by disarming assumptions, dogmas, prejudices—anything that makes us feel too safe and too confident. "Human wisdom is worth little or nothing," Socrates said at his trial in Athens, an assertion as unpalatable and subversive then as it is today. Abdoh, with wit and anger and compassion, persistently tore away the veneer with which society covers its ignorance and inadequacies. He understood that grappling with the conundrums of sex, identity, and death was not something to engage in as a means of learning answers or finding solutions, but rather as an end in itself, a never-ending, never-satisfying process that elevates humanity only insofar as it confronts our fallen condition with honesty, vulnerability, and resolve.

Note to the Introduction

1. In this context, *vertical* means simultaneous and *horizontal* means sequential. For a discussion of vertical and horizontal montage in Brecht's plays, see Martin van Dijk's "Blocking Brecht" in *Re-interpreting Brecht: His influence on Contemporary Drama and Film,* edited by Pia Kleber and Colin Visser.

Editor's Note

As is noted on the first page of the chronology, incorrect information has been printed in numerous publications about Abdoh's life prior to 1983. For various reasons, I've allowed biographical facts in articles reprinted here, now known to be false, to remain in the texts. Please consult the chronology for more accurate biographical information.

Omissions I made to excerpted texts are signified by bracketed ellipsis points. Unbracketed ellipsis points appeared in the original texts.

I Interviews

Josette Féral

Excerpts from "'Theatre Is Not about Theory':

An Interview with Reza Abdoh"

JF: What kind of training did you have?

RA: I went to the Youth Theatre in London when I was young and studied acting. Well, I didn't so much study acting. I was very young at the time. After that, really, my training was not in acting at all. It was mainly film, making my own theater pieces, studying dance, movement, stuff like that. I never had formal training for acting at all. [. . .]

JF: How do you choose your actors? On what premises, on what qualities do you base your selection?

RA: Ah! . . . Skill and talent, mainly. I'm a big fan of talent. That's very important to me. Versatility, courage—that's very important—fearlessness, lack of inhibition, I would say. Those are the main qualities that I think an actor should have. I don't think any actor really needs to be an intellectual in order to act. In fact, the less intellectual an actor is, the better. But if it is there with everything else, then it's even better. I have very intellectual actors, some of them are very, very intellectual. And they're very good actors. But I personally find the ones who have less intellectual obsessions more interesting because it seems like there's more force; sometimes they're more animalistic and less cerebral. . . . I mean, for me it's just a more powerful presence on stage.

JF: I'm asking these questions because there is a very anti-intellectual bias everywhere in North America. . . .

Originally published in *TDR* 39, no. 4 (T148) (Fall 1995): 86–96.

RA: Yes, there is. [. . .] In Europe, it's only intellectual, really. . . . In France, it's really something! There are very good actors there, but I don't think they could ever do my work. Well, they could if I really shaped them and reshaped them. I can understand where they are coming from because I also share that. But personally, I don't feel they are as good or as strong as actors, that they will do absolutely everything on stage, give their whole on stage. There's a lot of distance from these people. But they have tremendous skill, tremendous technique. But I feel, for example, when you're analyzing a text, a classical text mainly, it's a detriment to the final result, to the final production, to spend too much time analyzing it—because then there's no room for mystery or experiment or freedom; you have basically dried it from its core in a sense. I just don't agree with doing that. [. . .] I think text is an instrument to communicate on stage, and you can communicate in many different ways. If you specify exactly one way of doing it, then there is no room for mystery.

JF: How do you preserve the mystery?

RA: Well, for one thing, I make the work less strict. I mean in its relationship to the audience. I may have not said that at first but my work is very, very strict because it is completely choreographed.

JF: You mean it's not strict on the level of meaning?

RA: Yes. Artaud, for example, never believed that you should force meaning down an audience's throat. The most interesting people, really, in theater, didn't believe that. They always knew. Brecht, for example. I don't think any great artist believes that really. I think all really great, truly great artists in every medium, in every discipline, have always believed that in order to really communicate to their audience, they should allow some freedom of meaning, they should allow some space for a relationship between the audience and the work to take place, to take shape. [. . .]

JF: But on the other hand, the last performance I saw, *Tight Right White,* had a lot of explicit meaning. Would it be safe to say that you work on both levels?

RA: Of course. You have to communicate. As you might have noticed, I'm not an artist that only creates works that are formal. I just don't do that anymore. I don't believe in it. So, there are certain ideas that I also need to communicate, and in order to communicate them, aside from the visual language, you also need to communicate with words; and oftentimes it's impossible to communicate with your language, so you also have to create a kind of visual imagery, which for me is even more important in some cases. [. . .]

JF: I'd like to come back to acting, because you spoke a few minutes ago about "skills and talent." I'd very much like to know how that breaks down. (Laughter.) What are the qualities you are looking for in an actor?

RA: First of all, just on a very basic level, I like actors who know how to dance, how to use their voices. [. . .] Actually, I'm one of those directors who *does* think that technique is important. This technique—they surely have it before they arrive, of course. They come from different schools of acting. Most of the people I use are really professional actors. I mean, they have had this kind of training. But, I also work with complete nonprofessionals. For example, in this production [*Tight Right White*], three of the people in the play had never acted before; they're people who I felt had real presence and could act in one of my pieces. I like to combine the two. I like to combine people who are really highly trained with people who are not only not trained but also have never really acted before.

JF: But you still choose them based on certain characteristics.

RA: Well, I choose them for their presence mainly, and for their sense of themselves, and for the kind of freedom they might have; for a sense of a liberated kind of personality that might emanate from them. There are many reasons why one gets attracted to another person. I'm often looking for people who I either get inspired by or who I simply get to know or . . . who are real people, people who have lived in some way.

JF: [. . .] Louis Jouvet used to say, "Tel homme, tel acteur." [. . .] How would you define this "presence"?

RA: Freedom, I think. Just freedom to express without fear, freedom to reach out and connect with an audience, to make the audience feel something it has never really experienced before. I think a lot of that is really quite innate, but it's also about feeling confident with your skills and your abilities, to just basically get on that stage and make that connection. [. . . .] How does one really define a term like [*presence*]? It's not possible. It's one of those words in our language that we all know what it means, yet none of us can really define it. [. . .]

JF: Would you say that it has to do with concentration?

RA: With a sort of transcendent concentration probably. A great Noh performer once said that some student of his came to him and asked, "Master, great master, what were you thinking about in that moment of great beauty?" and he said, "Well, I was just thinking of when I'd need to put my left foot, at what point, so I wouldn't fall." I think that's like the quintessence of great acting, in a sense. That's the height of concentration.

JF: This brings me to another question: the relation of the actor to the character. In your plays, I wouldn't say that the actors impersonate the characters on a psychological level, but rather that they impersonate the main aspects of the character. How do you work on the characters?

RA: I subvert them in the way that I subvert text. Character to me is [. . .] a set of symbols and signs and [. . .] a psychological and emotional framework that a person inhabits, rather than a character that has an arc. [. . . S]ometimes it has an arc or it doesn't have an arc. Either it goes somewhere or it doesn't go anywhere. It's just like life, basically. I mean, you run across many different people that you don't know anything about, and they're characters in the grand novel of your life, but you never really get to know them. [. . .]

JF: So what kind of work does the actor do in terms of characterization? How do you ask actors to work on a character?

RA: I don't really think of it that way. I don't ask the actor to work on a particular character. I just think, well, there is a certain need that this persona has for the play to work. I call them personae rather than actors. In order to fulfill the total picture, you have to fulfill those requirements for that persona to work. You need to have a certain haircut, you need to have a certain walk, you need to have a certain voice, you need to have a certain relationship to the text, and you need to basically convey a certain set of emotional, intellectual, and physical connections to the audience so that the relationship is complete, because otherwise you're not communicating anything. But in total, the relationship is really the actual image itself of the characters. It is still quite abstract. A regular play, by Arthur Miller, let's say, can be defined in terms of character. There are no "real" characters in my work, but there are characters there. [. . .]

JF: You disrupt the character on several levels.

RA: Yes. In *Tight Right White* for instance, the piece you just saw, there are characters and there's a narrative, but it's continuously being disrupted and you're continuously questioning who is who, who is what, where. . . . That's really another way to throw into question the whole notion of character and plot.

JF: And you disrupt the characters to push the audience to reconstruct . . .

RA: To question . . . to question and reconstruct. Once you believe in a character, that's all you believe in from that point on. There's nothing else that you question. I think it's important to keep questioning.

JF: Is that your Brechtian influence?

RA: Probably. . . .

JF: Because it creates an alienation effect, it keeps the audience at a distance.

RA: Yes, maybe . . . [. . .]

JF: Your performances are always multimedia. They use a lot of technology. Why is technology so important to you?

RA: It offers a different point of view, a different perspective, a different expression. I'm expressing the same sort of ideas through those media. It also makes the story very abstract. It's much more abstract than the actual physical presence of actors on stage. And that's another way of subverting the expression, in a sense. But also, whether you like it or not, we live in a world that is absolutely filled with technology. It's unavoidable. I personally am for it. I like it and I approve of it and I want to use it in my work, because it not only helps to complement the work but it also helps to disrupt it, in a sense. For me that's very important, because it also puts into question that whole notion of perception, that whole notion of seeing, that whole notion of a connection to an idea, a message that is being provided on the TV screen.

JF: But there's no limit to disruption. How do you put a limit to disruption?

RA: The minute it starts to really destroy the essence of what it is that you're trying to say, it ceases to be disruptive, and it becomes destructive. [. . .]

JF: [. . . T]here is something common in all the plays: a certain violence, violence between people, violence towards the world, violence towards what's happening. Is that your way of seeing life?

RA: No . . . it's not the only way to see life, but it certainly is a very important way of seeing things. I think violence not only plays a very important part in our world, in our life, but it's also a form of reconstructing life in a sense. You don't just destroy through violence, you also recreate. A lot of writers have this idea. That's an idea that Dostoyevsky had, for example. But I wouldn't say it's the only way that I see the world. I mean, it's one of the ways I see it. The other one is more lyrical. Some of my work is very lyrical and funny. *Tight Right White* was a very funny play and *Quotations* was very lyrical in some ways.

JF: But we couldn't laugh, like in a farce.

RA: Well, no. Of course not. But who wants to laugh that way anymore anyway? I mean, I don't. I have a certain wit that is very specific.

JF: Would you say that this relation to violence is influenced by the fact that you live in the States?

RA: Shakespeare was the most violent playwright I know. His tragedies are filled with violence.

JF: That's true. . . . (Laughter.)

RA: [. . .] If I were living in Iran, obviously I would create like the Polish did, for example. The reason [their theater] was so strong was because it created a sense of truth, a sense of reality, where violence played a very important part, but it never really was violent. So I think with every culture, the practitioners of the art forms have an obligation to deal with the actual context of the culture, I mean with what is going on at the time. [. . .]

JF: Today spectators are not shocked when there is a naked actor on stage, but it's very difficult to make nakedness work. Your naked actors are quite often submitted to various forms of torture: in *Tight Right White* the actor was on a wheel, like in Leonardo da Vinci's design; in *Hip-Hop Waltz* he was tied, upside-down, while a giant drill headed towards his genitals.

RA: I'm very inspired by representations of dark forces in cultures, especially in medieval culture. Like images of Nazi Germany, images of real pain and suffering. I don't know why, but I've always been interested in the relationship between the dark forces and our psyche. I'm interested by the dark forces inside us. How does somebody kill six million people? What makes one make that decision to do acts of cruelty and butchery? I like to visualize that, "physicalize" that. I don't think it has anything really strange or really shocking in it anymore. Many artists have found that now. It's just *how* you do it, the form that it takes. That's important. [. . .]

JF: How do you think that theater can influence today's world, where communications systems are spreading rapidly and where the influence of art is very limited?

RA: In Sarajevo, from what I've heard, they put candles in basements and do theater, while from outside they're hearing sniper shots and people are getting shot. Theater is the only thing for them, to keep them from going mad. I still believe that theater has that possibility to let people in, to make them feel part of something. I do think theater should also pay attention to technology, and expand its own horizons and not get stuck. But I feel—and it's most fundamental above all—that theater is still a place where people can share ideas and feel safe in a sense, or not feel safe, or feel insecure as the case might be. And a fine example is, of course, countries where there's massive repression, and yet people come together for an hour to share an experience. That's one of the main reasons I do theater. Obviously, I don't live in a repressed country—to a certain extent repressed but not in the same ways that Sarajevo is—so, of course, my relationship to my work is not fundamentally driven as it necessarily would be there. But still, that's one of the reasons. Theater for me is also a personal quest. It's a personal journey. It's not a religion. It's a way for me to express my own desires and . . . feelings, and pains . . . and memories.

Hortensia Völckers and Martin Bergelt

Excerpts from "Violence—Death—Theatre"

HV, MB: In your piece *The Law of Remains* you combine very different elements: on the one hand the Egyptian *Books of Death,* on the other hand Andy Warhol, and both with the man-eating mass murderer Jeffrey Dahmer, whose crimes have only recently been cleared up. What is the connection between these subjects that seem to be so very different?

RA: In one word: death. A kind of obsessive yearning for bodily existence beyond Death. A problem that preoccupies our culture to a great extent, that torments the body and in doing so makes the problem evident. You can see that every day on TV: the usage of the body as a means of demonstrating eternal youth. I call it the excoriation of the body, a kind of release of the body from all defects, as it is shown to us for example by the cosmetics commercials. This is an obsession by which especially the American culture is affected. The culture seems to be addicted to death since it is always trying to somehow deny it.

HV, MB: So is there a kind of correspondence between the Egyptian mummies, the deep-frozen body of an American hoping to be revived in the future, the frozen time in the film, and on the other side a person like Jeffrey Dahmer confronting the parts of the body, the decomposing remains, in a shocking way?

RA: Yes, that's right. With my theater I criticize the established culture models which deny death in its materiality by portraying, for example, one of those confused people whose actions do not fit into the sublimation model. But in addition to this cultural and socio-critical orien-

1. Originally published in *Theaterschrift*, no. 3 (1993): 48–65.

23

tation, I am also looking for a philosophical path that is not prescribed, that in its openness might lead into darkness and destruction, too, but that in any case does not have a direction which is prescribed by means of cultural prohibition signs. In my opinion the important feature of my work is that it constantly questions the patriarchy, the patriarchal domination of any kind of discussion about religion, society, political structures, etc. The prescribed models can neither serve me as an artist nor the people being dominated. That is the political aspect.

HV, MB: And the philosophical one?

RA: Philosophically I am interested for example in the strange schizophrenia in the moral evaluation of violence and destruction. Both of them are wearing the sign "taboo." But that is completely untrustworthy, since the entire progress of our culture is based on violence and destruction.

HV, MB: You mean that evolution is understood too idealistically? Without violence and destruction, no history?

RA: Yes, because actually violence was and is still being used and glorified. None of us is completely innocent. When the U.S.A. starts the Gulf War, no matter for what reason, violence is legalized. And in political rhetoric all this is celebrated as a victory of good over evil. But how can one say that an act of violence which is committed in the street is less moral than the killing of hundreds of thousands of Arabs? That's schizophrenic. The whole sense of the moral argument seems to consist in disguising the act of violence or destruction. In our culture, violence is always sanctioned in the name of progress, which clearly demonstrates that it is not morality that counts but domination.

HV, MB: Let's talk about Jeffrey Dahmer. His acts of violence cannot be justified even if he is considered an aberrant terminator. Dahmer is homosexual, doing violence exclusively to colored people he had sexual contact with. The courts consider him sane. Where does this fatal chain of violence and sexuality stem from?

RA: Jeffrey Dahmer is a by-product of the stigmatization which is regarded as normal in this society. This man repressed his origin, his sexuality, his entire ego, thus obeying a ruling model of self-repression.

Dahmer is an unskilled worker, he is a homosexual, he feels attracted to colored people—stigmas wherever you look. Between his ego and his superego a vehement tension came into existence to which Jeffrey Dahmer responded with destruction, because nobody who was taught to repress sexuality is able to love. After being arrested, it's not his murders that he denies but his homosexuality, which is typical. In prison he called the black people "niggers" and the Latinos "spics" and said that they deserved to die, although he felt sexually attracted to people of a different color. What becomes clear is that Dahmer cannot accept his own ego. In this case it is not a private demon but a product of the collective American superego that determines in its absolutism what's right and what's wrong. [. . .]

HV, MB: You are an advocate of the catharsis theory. Do you believe in the purifying force of the enacted shock?

RA: I believe in it not so much as a purifying of emotion, but as a celebration of it. I don't want to send the audience through purgatory but to create a solemn atmosphere of emotion. You know, the Tibetans take their dead to the mountain top, chop them up, and use them as feed. For a Westerner [. . .] that is unacceptable because it goes against every moral sense that you have. But to the Tibetans it is an act of redemption, of purity. They are perfectly aware that they are chopping up flesh. They are under no illusions that after death the body is anything more than just a piece of meat. Only when illusions take over—like in our body-fixated society that is not familiar with transcendence—the situation becomes problematic. In the Western world, death is not accepted as a condition of the body, but regarded as a defect, a construction fault.

HV, MB: Perhaps it might be said that Dahmer's sexually motivated cannibalism represents a—perversely heightened—expression of exactly that Western fixation on just the pure body? Where there is no spiritual dimension, love may be perverted to possession of the body and then literally to the consumption of it.

RA: Yes—and the macabre end is—as becomes clear at the end of my play—nothing more than a plate with bones. End of the illusions.

HV, MB: Your theater has a shocking effect. You work with the means of cruelty and pornography. Is shock a means of reaching the audience?

RA: [. . . S]hock for me is not a method but at best the result of a recognition. Theater has a lot more potential. I think theater is really a place to physicalize ideas, a kind of a forum to exchange ideas.

Howard Ross Patlis

Dark Shadows and Light Forces

HRP: Do you find beauty in violence?

RA: Yeah. In violence and in dark elements, I find a sort of rigor and a vigor that is moving for me, therefore it's beautiful.

HRP: *The Law of Remains* confronts its viewers with so much information so rapidly that it seems impossible for one to process not only what is going on but what one is experiencing. Is this intended?

RA: I like my work to be very dense, and I like not to necessarily destroy but to question the validity of theatrical conventions that say you need to relent or make certain modulations at a certain point, or that you need to orchestrate something in a particular way in order for it to work or affect an audience. All this is accumulated wisdom from 2500 years ago, and I can either choose to accept it or to question it and dissolve it. I often choose to dissolve it in my work.

HRP: Does hate drive the work?

RA: There's . . . space for it, but it doesn't drive it. It's a longing for something more humane, and a longing for a dream, sort of, for something that is a model or a paradigm that is more useful to a people for whom the existing models do not suffice. [. . .]

HRP: Can showing the violent images and filling our image repertoire with negativity help us? Do you think of the images as positive?

RA: I don't think of things as positive and negative, I just think of them as holistic, as part of the holistic framework, the holistic tapestry of our psyche, our universe.

HRP: During the performance [of *The Law of Remains*] there is a lot of violence acted out toward women. In the opening image, as the audience walks in, we see a woman hanging from a noose. Later, a strangling scene from a Hitchcock film is viewed and then re-enacted by the performers. Is this a critique of male oppression, and if so, how does the spectator know that it's a critique?

RA: There's no way the spectator will definitely know. In my work, often it's the patriarchal figures that are the cause of the mayhem and it's the anima, the feminine, that in some way creates a path toward afterlife or some kind of salvation. And this is probably not without exception. . . . The feminine part of my nature exists in the work much stronger in some ways, because I believe in the Dionysian forces.

HRP: Is it possible to make the critique clear that you are not merely staging a reproduction of violence toward women?

RA: It is a reproduction of violence toward women . . . but also toward men. No, because I'm not that interested in making things too clear. It's a poeticization, not a documentation.

HRP: In poeticizing this subject, do you feel you run the risk of allowing for a degree of ambiguity that would become potentially dangerous ethically? It's a question of responsibility. Walter Benjamin defined a fascist aesthetic as one that detaches its form from its content, or, in the case of Nazi Germany, beautifying war and acts of violence. Could this be applied to your work?

RA: No. [. . .] The work is way too passionate for that to happen. This whole critique of work that is not linear, that purports content is sacrificed for form, is irrelevant in this kind of work. It doesn't mean anything, you know, because the line between form and content just doesn't exist. There is no such line. At least not in the kind of work I'm interested in. Yes, in conventional theatrical representations, in plays, that matters. But in this kind of work, which is more music, more dance than a play, that sort of definition does not suffice.

HRP: How does dance function in the piece?

RA: Like joints. If you think of a metaphor for the body, it would be joints—connecting tissues. [. . .]

HRP: There are many points in the performance when an actor will stab or shoot and kill another player. This also seems to hold a dancelike and vaudevillian quality. Both people involved in the incident usually fall, or die together.

RA: This represents how I think of an act of violence. The prey and the predator are in a marriage in some way and both destroy and create each other at the same time.

HRP: Do you think of your theater as radical or avant-garde?

RA: No, I don't. It may adhere to certain radical conventions that have existed before me, but I don't think of anything as radical anymore. In this day and age to think of anything as radical is presumptuous, and not just presumptuous but so fake. What's radical is in the streets, the war in Iraq is radical. . . . The avant-garde no longer exists. Those lines don't exist anymore. People who go to Broadway come see my work and vice versa. And the people who go see the Metropolitan Opera will very rarely come see my work, but those lines are not what's important.

HRP: In section 4, the performers move to a playing space behind a chain link fence that initially made up the stage-left wall. All the dialogue spoken by the actors during this part is lip-synched to the sounds of the actors' voices on tape. To take away the actor's voice is potentially a totalitarian act.

RA: Yes, it's a very totalitarian act, it is. But the tension between that and the need to get out, to get away from it, to break through the body, the fence, the language barrier, because language in this sense doesn't represent the psyche, it imprisons it, in a way. Because the desire to break out, to break through is so much stronger than the need to be responsive to the task at hand. That tension interests me.

HRP: How did the idea to lip-synch the whole section occur?

RA: I'm personally fascinated by a vision of the world in which nobody speaks anymore, where everybody is programmed to speak, that language simply fails our thoughts, our feelings, our dreams, our memories. I'm also interested in the campy, B-movie, pop-culture conventions that it represents. I'm interested in movie as a form of reproduction of an image, of a thought, of an idea, and of a language—that it's always filtered, no matter what. It will have, always, gone through an editing facility.

HRP: Is the act of presenting homoerotic acts on stage motivated at all by an impulse to bring gay sex from the margins of society to the eyes of mainstream audiences?

RA: Well, I'm queer and I don't think of myself as marginalized. And I hope queers around the world don't think of themselves as marginalized, even though they do. I think we have tremendous power politically, financially, artistically.

HRP: In one part of "Heaven," as many of the performers are at the edge of their cots (that look like hospital beds of an early-twentieth-century mental institution), they thrust one arm down between their legs and their faces light up in an expression of horror or surprise—

RA: —or pleasure—

HRP: —or pleasure. It brought to my mind the linkage that the AIDS crisis has formed between that area of the body, our second chakra, and death.

RA: Yes, exactly, that the AIDS crisis links literal death to this area, that pleasure is banned for us because the cock, vagina, or asshole was the cause in some way. So pleasure seeking is somehow equated with that; desire—fulfillment of desire—is equated with that. And that is something that I think is negligent and irresponsible.

HRP: Can you explain?

RA: The desexualization of victims—of AIDS, cancer, rape victims, incest victims—is something society does to manifest the horror of people who are experiencing those troubles. And that to me is . . . fascistic, a form of thought-body control that is very cruel and unjust . . . and that is done all the time. On TV, you see AIDS victims who are withering away on a bed and right after that, you see a commercial of big boobs selling beer. The juxtaposition of those two images derails our psyche [so] that we can never think of that withered man on the bed as a sexual object, but we can very clearly associate beer with sexuality. That's sort of a common practice in our popular culture.

HRP: What is it you want to communicate to your audience?

RA: (Long pause.) That it's not enough to think of a world that is more livable . . . but that you have to act on it.

Philippa Wehle

Excerpts from

"Reza Abdoh and *Tight Right White*"

PW: How do you go about creating a piece? Where do you start?

RA: I become excited about an issue or a subject matter or a thought, something I've read in a newspaper or book or article, or seen on TV, or something I might have experienced myself personally. These issues [in *Tight Right White*]—prejudice, and a kind of quest for identity—are things that are very personal for me. And the way I come to terms with my questions is to explore them in my mind. [. . .]

PW: What are the sources this time? I know you've mentioned *White on Black: Images of Africa and Blacks in Western Culture,* by Jan Nederveen Pieterse.

RA: Yes, these sources were inspirational. And I've adapted the book/film *Mandingo.* That's pretty much it. The rest is my own work. *Wake Up Dead Man,* the collection of chain gang songs was inspirational. "Wake up dead man" appears several times in the play. What that phrase evokes inspires me. And contemporary popular culture, slave narratives, new Nazi manifestoes, TV, stuff like that. I'm sort of like a receiver, and I filter all this information to write the final thing. [. . .]

I'm not a poser of ideas. I'm certainly not a journalist. I'm certainly not after presenting any clear-cut answers. I pose a lot of questions. . . . It's a form of longing for some kind of response, some kind of legitimate solution. . . . But it is never done heavy-handedly. The most important

Originally published in *Theatreforum,* no. 4 (Winter/Spring 1994): 60–62.

part of my aesthetic, in my writing at least, is my "gallows humor," and that's something that I cherish. It's part of me.

PW: What made you choose the Jewish wedding dance and the Austrian dance, I mean in relationship to the theme.

RA: They connect to something ancient. And the Alpine dance, there's a lot of Germanic imagery in the play with the neo-Nazi ideas. And the Jewish wedding dance is the idea of union, the idea of renewal, of regeneration. There are also contemporary dances, street dances, funky and hip-hop. Those, of course, are forms that give expression to rage, to unity, again, a sense of community. Like Kathakali, each gesture represents an idea, a thought, a theme. The same thing with contemporary house dances. House music is a contemporary form that urban kids do. It's like eurhythmics. Their gestures, it's a language they communicate with. It's a code. The underground culture has to have a codified language. That's what I do in my work, I think. There's a kind of codified language, like between Blaster and the Master of Ceremonies [also called Moishe Pipik]. All these codes keep popping up.

PW: Is it a problem for you if your audience doesn't know the film *Mandingo*?

RA: It's not so much interesting to me for people to understand everything. If people don't understand anything of my ninety-minute production, if they haven't grasped a sliver of a story, then there's something wrong with them. But no, it doesn't make it more rich to have seen the film, because first of all, it's not about the film. The *Mandingo* track is a springboard. I haven't set out to stage *Mandingo*.

Language is a ready-made tool of communication. It's a set of shared symbols, a form of repression. So, not to understand everything or not to share all the symbols is perfectly OK for me; in fact, it helps my work, because the work becomes more a puzzle rather than something that's easily digestible.

John Bell

Excerpts from "To Reach Divinity through

the Act of Performance: An Interview with

Reza Abdoh"

JB: What other theater had you been exposed to at the time you performed in Robert Wilson's *KA MOUNTAIN, GUARDenia TERRACE* [1972, at the age of nine] in Iran?

RA: Well, it's really misleading to say "performed" in *KA MOUNTAIN*. I was just an extra. That's one thing which needs to be clarified. It really always bugs me when people write that. And the other thing is, I was exposed to theater. I mean, I'd seen theater, I'd seen Peter Brook's *Midsummer Night's Dream* [1971], which I thought was heavenly. That was the main thing that I was probably really impressed by, Peter Brook. [. . .]

JB: How do you feel about avant-garde theater as a tradition that includes people like Mallarmé and Jarry, Duchamp, and later Brook and Wilson? How do you respond when people say, about your work or avant-garde work in general, "Oh, that's been done before"?

RA: It probably has. I think that's just a facile way of saying "I don't get this; and I don't want to admit that I don't get it so I'm just going to say it's been done before." What kind of bullshit is that? So what—everything has been done before. [. . .]

JB: Does the term *postmodern* in any way define your work?

RA: I've always had a problem with that. I don't think so really. I think "postmodern" is an easy way to describe something you don't understand. And I think my work doesn't really include a lot of the theories

Originally published in *TDR* 39, no. 4 (T148) (Fall 1995): 48–71.

that would define a work as postmodern. It doesn't even agree with them, because it has a point of view. And one of the major facets of postmodernism is that you shouldn't have a point of view. But I definitely have a point of view in my work, a very strong point of view, both political and social, and aesthetic. But if you read Derrida or many of the important philosophers of postmodernism, one of the most important aspects of it is that there is no absolutism, and I just don't believe that. But, having said that, I admire some of the work. Derrida has influenced me quite a bit, Foucault certainly has: his writing, and actually his life too. [. . .]

JB: In what major ways have your shows changed?

RA: They're more mature. I've found my own voice, my own aesthetic. I give a lot more attention to clarity and sharpness and discipline on stage. I think when I did *Medea* that was the real change, the seeds of my present aesthetic. It started developing staging, multimedia; it threw away linear narratives; I started becoming interested in using different cultural traits. [. . .]

JB: Sometimes you hear the same line repeated throughout a show, like "You're going to make a heap of money from this movie," in *The Law of Remains,* and "We are searching for a gem of a tale to tell on TV," in *Tight Right White.* What do you get from this technique of using text?

RA: Well, first of all I think it plugs into this sort of maniacal obsession in today's media-saturated world to drive a message by any means possible and to keep repeating it and repeating and repeating it till we get so saturated with it that it somehow transforms itself into a subliminal message. And there are certain structural patterns that I try to create. Often when I structure my work I think of musical forms; a fugue, for example. In a Bach fugue there's a phrase that can get repeated several million times and each time it gets repeated there's a little variety. I feel that's effective as a way of communication. When I listen to Bach, the structure is so, in a sense, perfect, and the contrapuntal quality about it—it seems to all just fall in the right place. [. . .]

JB: When you're working with images do you figure them all out beforehand, like Robert Wilson, or do you work on them with the group and then change the juxtapositions to see what they come up with?

RA: Both. Sometimes I think of certain images in connection to text. Sometimes I think of certain images in connection with music. And sometimes I just think of images for their own power and poignancy. And as I develop the work, of course, like a painter who uses paint, I use actors and lights. [. . .]

JB: Why is all the text in *Quotations,* except for Mario's monologues and a couple of other minor things, lip-synched?

RA: So I could have complete control.

JB: Is that something you want to do in the future, shows that are completely lip-synched?

RA: Not necessarily. I did it in this one because I wanted to experiment. It is about experimentation. If you don't experiment, you're going to die, basically; your work will get stale. I want to experiment with the idea of distancing the performer from the text, so you don't get too bogged down by interpretation. [. . .]

JB: *The Law of Remains* had many different types of dance; *Tight Right White* was almost a history of various dance forms. This is very different from a choreographer who invents their own choreography.

RA: I'm not really a big fan of a lot of modern dance. Some of it is great, but a lot of it is very empty. But I really admire, respect, and have a great affection for indigenous dance forms. In *Law of Remains* I used a lot of West African dance, American musical forms (which is actually the one dance form that I have the deepest affection for), and tap. In the current piece [*Quotations*] I use some Middle Eastern dancing and, again, some American musical dance. I'm always searching for those indigenous forms of dance that are really in danger of extinction, I'd say. And I, of course, give them a twist. I don't just use them as a cultural tourist, as it were; I manipulate them.

JB: Speaking about the dances as indigenous forms makes them function almost like objects to be considered or admired. In *Quotations,* do the video and film images, music pieces, slang phrases, and visual elements, like the Puritan or Boy Scout costumes, function in the same way?

RA: More or less, yes; they all create this tapestry. You don't sit down and say, "Oh this does this, that does that"—you sit down and just watch it; it's like a poem. When you're reading a poem, your first impression is not "This line represents this." Eventually, you start analyzing it. But the whole purpose of creating the use of different media, the different vocabularies—from dance, to music, to video—is to create a landscape that is made hyper, that goes beyond ordinary reality, beyond mundane. [. . .]

JB: There seems to be some kind of political philosophy imbedded in *Quotations*. Could you describe it?

RA: I believe that one has to not be a victim.

Thomas Leabhart

Excerpts from "Reza Abdoh," an Interview

(The interviewer omitted his questions in the original publication.)

Los Angeles has a unique concave and convex reality which happens at the same time, where many cultures are running on parallel tracks, maintaining their own identities, but at the same time meshing to assimilate with the dominant culture. In other places I've worked that's not always true. [. . .] Sometimes the dominant culture is too strong and has overwhelmed them, or the other cultures have intentionally not tried to maintain their individual identities.

New York is a unique case; there is an artistic tradition of dialogue between an audience and a creator which is lacking in California, and that dialogue between the creator and the viewer determines how a work is perceived and the direction that it takes. On the other hand, in New York there is a pre-formed set of rules, expectations, a norm or paradigm that you either try to uphold or try to break. When people go to see something they are always referring back to that model. There is a long tradition, especially in the performing arts, in New York. Here, in Los Angeles, that tradition simply does not exist.

I feel that the environment in L.A. enriches me; the unpredictability of it fuels my work. The aesthetic one forms here has the potential of becoming one's own aesthetic, as one is not necessarily conforming to a certain trend or an existing paradigm. In other places there is a push toward conforming to a certain model. There still remains a frontier spirit here. It's ironic, because in the pop culture there is very much an emphasis on trend making, whereas in the sub-pop world, or in the subcultures, there is a frontier spirit.

Popular culture is the livelihood of this country, and a lot of it gets manufactured in Hollywood, because Hollywood is the apex of the industry of image making. Image making is equal to economic power and economic subjugation; popular culture is not just about what is being sold on television, but about how your thought is being processed for you, how your thought is being determined. A great deal of that is manufactured here. The marginality of the subcultures is something that you either believe or you don't. If you believe that you are marginal, then indeed you are. It is important to think about how subcultures affect the popular culture. The relationship is one of a vulture feeding on remains. A great deal of popular culture is a result of what happens in subculture. Open a stylish magazine; the images that protrude are the result of what has happened in the last seventy years in the subculture. The trick is to break one's own rules so one does not become a consumer product, a prisoner of one's own conventions. Is it worthwhile to attempt to create a work that remains religious, a work that links one to the higher aspect of one's self? That effort is worthwhile, whether it is successful or not. James Joyce spent his life writing a book which is incomprehensible, and remains an enigma and a phenomenon of the twentieth century. Was it worthwhile? Yes.

The original impulse behind *The Hip-Hop Waltz of Eurydice* was my gut reaction to systematic repression and erosion of freedom taking place around me. Instead of feeling helpless about it I decided to create a piece. I think on a multitrack; I never think mono. Art today needs to have a holistic nature; it's not the time for an atomistic, Newtonian approach to art. I don't believe in creating work that is too easily digestible. It's important to create work that resonates in every aspect of one's personal and universal self. That impulse grew into different aspects of the piece. *Hip-Hop* summarizes what my struggle has been with my work in the last eight years or so. There are certain themes, certain preoccupations, certain obsessions, dreams, nightmares that I've had continuously which somehow were tied together in this piece, but not necessarily resolved.

A spiritual pigeonholing takes place in this culture; it is a feeling of my God as opposed to your God. Spiritual entrapment is shown in the spear shaking of morality in the name of decency. What is decent is to care about people, not to thumbtack them on the wall and say "This is this and that is that." The mechanism of spiritual entrapment is important to the piece. The language of the piece conveys a verbal fascism that this culture continuously but very subtly lays on us, lays on itself really. The logorrhea that results is a defense mechanism that we like to use as a weapon. The tension between language and the body is shown in the way the body is made as an object of desire but an object that is memory, that is present but is also a memory, in the same way that language is an object which is also present yet a memory. How is that controlled? In [the "Hell" section], the relationship of the thought to the spoken word is shown in the way the body is moving continuously toward an imaginary and an actual fence and keeps bumping into it and keeps getting shoved back. Ultimately what happens is that the unity of the body, thought, and language breaks through the wall. It tries to refute the notion of dualism, the instance of either/or, the belief in Aristotelian, Christian dualism. There is the possibility of cracking the binary system and replacing it with a holistic approach. In "Hell," where the psyche of Orpheus, the psyche of Eurydice, and the psyches of the slaves interact, the language that you're hearing is at once the language that is being spoken functionally, language as a function, and language that is being spoken in order to subjugate, language of communication, language of support, language of memory. But at the same time you are hearing a language that has nothing to do with any of these functions but is a language of the spirit. It ties into the history of the spirit rather than a history of material events. The history of the spirit ties into the language of the body as a function: it shits, it eats, it pisses, it fucks. [. . .] All these themes become united and embodied by the slaves, by the hounds, by Eurydice, and by Orpheus, and are opposed by the character of the Captain, a fascist undertaker-overtaker of the underworld. When they come head to head, the wall breaks, opening the possibility of renewal, of a new birth, of love.

How does one embody abstract thought and physicalize ideas that are the essentials? This seems to be the most important question in theater. How does one manifest the invisible and the unknown without making it into a property? In order for this to happen, the performers have to become primary creators. It is essential to think of the performer as a primary creator in this process, because the act of becoming another person is not as urgent. What is of concern is to re-establish one's contact with an inner matrix which might not be at the forefront of one's consciousness. In order for this contact to be made, the process needs to break down and regenerate continuously.

I've know these actors for a long time, and they're important to my work. Casting takes place without one's being conscious of it. Somehow it manifests itself in all its uniqueness and one does not have any choice. One sees it there. For the character of Captain, who embodies fascism, the dark nature, I wanted an actor who had savvy, coolness. I always wondered why people play Lady Macbeth so viciously, when it's more interesting to me if she appears benign; horrendous acts come out of her. Captain needed to be a poet, a Baudelaire, but grosser; he needed to be physically repellent. There's a moment when he talks about his complete loneliness, desperately clinging to a notion of immortality. There are those aspects of the character which could only be conveyed through an actor who had experienced these things but had repressed them at the same time, but who also had the technique and the savvy to convey it. In the cases of Orpheus and Eurydice, it was important to de-gender the play so it didn't become about the tensions of men-women, men-men, women-women but was instead about the universal conflicts and specific conflicts that we deal with constantly on a human level, and about the kind of gender roles that are dictated to us. I needed to amplify and to emphasize those. The way to do that was to reverse the roles of the characters.

The quotidian movement that opens the play—Eurydice is chopping vegetables, Orpheus is typing—that reality, the surface reality, is a parallel text to the sur-reality, the higher reality, the super-consciousness that manifests itself through the movement of the *capoeira* dancers. There is an id, and under-reality, a sub-conscious reality that manifests itself primarily through the activities of the underworld, but it also manifests itself through the movement of the *capoeira* dancers. Certain everyday gestures are filled with psychic energy; body movement, gesture has a psychic history, a reservoir that comes with it. Certain quotidian gestures have that reservoir, which one is not aware of. Motion is the one element in the human history which connects us to light, to space, and to history. In the piece, motion operates by conveying those three layers of reality simultaneously.

[. . .] I'm involved with the use of different media in theater rather than working purely theatrically. Media work has certain impulses which recognize the force that drives life into certain areas that become significantly mundane, like the rotten fruits of St. Augustine. Light, space, and motion interact through different media. The use of the rear-screen video in *Hip-Hop* hooks you into the psyche of the world outside as well as the psyche of the world inside. When the Captain throws the coffin through the window, you see a world that shatters. The boy behind the window represents the forces behind the window, which are facing us but which we choose not to see. At the start of the play, the figure behind the window, which was before reproduced, is now, at the end of the play, alive. That is translated through light into space, and in space translated to motion. On one level it is completely reproduced, it is not actual; on another level, it's actual, and that is only possible when you are using different media.

[. . .] Before [*Pasos en la Obscuridad*], I did a piece in New York entitled *Father Was a Peculiar Man*. The title was taken from vaudeville, which interests me a great deal. I took nineteenth-century psychological realism and mixed it with vaudeville and American music hall. I'm influenced by reading about vaudeville, and also by television performers of the 1950s who were vaudevillians: Jack Benny, Gracie Allen, Art Carney, Jackie Gleason. My hero is Buster Keaton, one of the great American artists. In fact, he is a character in *Father Was a Peculiar Man*. The point of departure for *Father* is *The Brothers Karamazov;* it deals with the family as a degenerating unit. We were dealing with things I'm obsessed with, like the killing of authority, in several different stages. The trajectory of the piece started with the killing of the father, patricide in the family, Karamazov; then, the killing of the king, the president, the assassination of JFK; then the killing of God, in the crucifixion. In the end there was a redemptive act, when after the crucifixion the audience and the actors sang "Dream a Little Dream" together. There were sixty performers, an entire marching band, and it took place in four street blocks of the meatpacking district in New York. It is an area of cobblestone streets, abandoned storefronts, and meat warehouses; it is very dark and it's all about what is happening behind closed doors in the psychic underbelly of the streets. The piece took place in some abandoned slaughterhouses where you could still see the dry, brown ash which remained from the blood that had been spilled there. That's where the vision of heaven and hell was created. The characters were J. F. Kennedy, Jackie O., Buster Keaton, Karamazov.

This piece played with '60s icons and the notion of icon making. It is now time for iconoclasm, time to destroy the myths we create to have something to cling to. We need to separate ourselves from then, break the icons, break the myths so that there is a possibility for renewal.

The unification of the spirit, the body, and the person is something that mystic poets write about and something I'm obsessed with. I hope to come to that one day. But there must be a purgation before certain psychic tumults can be cleansed. Until then, the chaos, the destruction, is necessary. The Hindus believe in the *Kali* age, an age of destruction. This is important in order to make us aware of our responsibility to ourselves and our need to align ourselves with something which is less about our material selves and more about our spiritual ones. I say this unabashedly. It's the vogue now to believe that nature is a fake, that there is no nature, and I understand why there is a need to believe that; but even that is a paradox, because if you believe that nature is a fake, that there is no absolute truth, then simply by the act of believing you are refuting the belief that there is no belief. The sheer fact that you have the capacity to imagine a genesis, a beginning, makes it real. There is a there there.

Andréa R. Vaucher

Excerpts from an Interview with Reza Abdoh

(The interviewer omitted her questions in the original publication.)

The very first thing I did after I found out I was HIV positive was a video called "Sleeping with the Devil." I became a lot more conscious of the body, the excoriation of the body as a tool. And I consciously, or unconsciously, infused the piece with that idea. I'm preoccupied with the body and with shit and cum and all the other stuff. I like to concentrate on excavation, excretion, things like that. I think it has something to do with the diagnosis. But I don't think I'm concerned with that only because of my condition. There are a number of ideas and concepts I'm concerned with and excited by that aren't necessarily linked to my condition. But my condition informs me, my psyche, my mentality, my sexuality, my being. It's not something that I can look away from or put on the sidelines or not make a part of, in some way, everything I do.

I've become much more aware of action as opposed to passivity. I've become much more interested in active participation in forming your life, your destiny. Before, I was less politically and socially motivated.

Anger is in my work as a cleansing agent. I don't mean that in a pedantic way, not as a cleansing agent that is cathartic or purging. I mean anger as an agent that propels you to take action. To write down your own rules, to make your own rules, to create your own universe. Why should I embrace [society's] constructs? Why should I look up at

Portions of what follows were included in Vaucher's *Muses from Chaos and Ash: AIDS, Artists, and Art* (New York: Grove Press), 1993. The interview was conducted on October 11, 1991.

it as this formidable paradigm that will save me? There's no reason. I have to derail it. I have to create my own.

AIDS has created a landscape in which the body and the spirit, and the politic of the body and the spirit, can be examined, reshaped, restructured, destroyed, and reformed. I think it's important for us as a people who are not embracing the status quo to discover our own road to what you might want to call redemption or salvation. It has nothing whatsoever to do with the Judeo-Christian idea of salvation or redemption. It has to do with a certain kind of peace that you find within yourself and you transmit hopefully through a generous act to your community. I think the queer community has managed to come to some kind of an understanding of that need for discovery.

It comes into [my] work first and foremost through the channels that I deal with, my conscious and subconscious channels. It works itself through in subliminal ways. Everything I do in some way deals with the notion of restructure, restructuring of something that has been destroyed, something that has been either intentionally destroyed or destroyed by means beyond your power. So of course death and redemption and ecstasy and structures of family which are laden with unexamined concepts—it's a way of looking at these things and thinking, "How do we reshape these, how do we look at them again? How do we create a way of accepting who we are in our own image rather than in someone else's?" That's something that my work deals with over and over. And the struggle with faith, blind faith. The struggle with the surrender to faith that I have, personally. [There's] an oppressive anti-humanism that takes over the consciousness when you're dealing with certain issues, or when you're looking at the kind of life that is perpetuating those ideas.

I'd like to write a novel. A piece that is narrative, that is long. I want to try to work with several narratives at once, with something that is not a visual medium in any way. Where the image is all suppressed. In the past couple of years I've become more—not attached, necessarily—but consumed and seduced by language. And I want to try to de-seduce myself. For one thing we allow ourselves to be seduced, and I think the folly that language puts forward is so laden with subterfuge. You can lay something out in language and the text can destroy itself, and then what you read becomes something that is completely alien to the subjective meaning. Text and pleasure have many things in common, least of which is comfort and the most important of which is subterfuge.

Deterioration of the body, I don't connect with shock. It might arouse compassion or pity in people. It might arouse revulsion or self-pity, fear of what happens if I look that way. It's a tragic way of responding to decay which has nothing whatsoever to do with a genuine response. It has everything to do with: "I will feel this way because after I have felt this way I can put that feeling away and move on." I think a lot of people's response when it comes to decay, deterioration, destruction is calculated. I don't think it's genuine most of the time. Basically, people are so accustomed to seeing, witnessing, hearing about atrocity, that decay and destruction and deterioration of the body or mind is not something that is going to affect them on a level beyond how they connect to a thirty-second news item about some impoverished country or the local news. The mediated information has calcified people's imaginations and people's reflexes and responses.

The genuine response is a response that has in some way managed to de-detach itself from the experience. I wouldn't say to attach, that's too much to hope for. The audience comes in ready to detach. Especially in theater, because the event is physically first of all removed from them, and psychically it's happening on a plane that is beyond their immediate reach. So it's subliminal. So when the experience forces them, or invites them, to de-detach themselves from what they are witnessing, then I think the relationship of the viewer to the event is a genuine relationship. And they can interpret it, they can read it in certain different ways. They can emotionally respond to it. They can become a part of it. They can hate it. They can think it's crap, whatever. But it's impossible for them to be in a state of stasis. So it's movement that I'm after. An infusion of a radical or a subtle shift in their perception. [. . .]

New ideas are coming because the experience is new. Basically, my thoughts are the same. Someone said you're always writing the same book or painting the same painting but every time it's so radically shifted that you can't possibly say it's the same thing. And in the same way, my film embodies what I'm thinking about, what I'm concerned with, not just my aesthetic but what I'm concerned with in life. What I'm finding out here is that the piece is about what's outside and what's inside. What's outlined and separates the two. How you go from one to the other. How you reshape one in order to enter into the other or vice versa. And that of course can denote many things. It can denote the living and the dead. It can denote outside of the window and inside the window, it can denote what's on your face as opposed to what's inside it. And I'm finding that the film is depicting more and more that sort of a relationship in its poetics and in its language and in its politics, story.

I think the impulse to redefine yourself because of an agent that is invading you is a very strong impulse. But I think it has been important for me not to permit that redefinition as a tool for self-pity or a tool for a self-discovery that detaches me from myself, from my body, from my pleasures, from my pains, from my sex, from my psyche, from my spirit. So whatever redefinition needs to occur, I think it needs to occur not because AIDS or HIV is the manipulating agent, but because AIDS or HIV are forces that you reckon with and then you wake up and find the strength to allow yourself and the community that you are part of to see the force and realize that force.

II Script

The Hip-Hop Waltz of Eurydice

At five minutes to curtain, JULIANA *enters, dressed as Orpheus/Tommy, and sits in chair. She chooses a woman to be the "blue lady," giving her the "blue lady ribbon." Then she returns to her chair and sits. At curtain,* TOM, *dressed as Eurydice/Dora Lee, enters with a towel. He crosses to the chair, takes out a straight razor, and begins to sharpen it on a leather strop. He strops faster and faster, until the bell sounds, at about thirty seconds after curtain.* TOM *puts shaving foam from a mug onto* JULIANA'*s face, then shaves her. As* TOM *does a final stroke, removing a hair from her upper lip, a bell sounds.*

JULIANA *crosses to bed, pulls out a manual typewriter, places it on the bed, and begins to type. The keys jam occasionally, and she pulls them back.* TOM *strikes chair off stage right. Crosses to shelf, and begins filling the kettle and pot with water. He places the bucket under the faucet and begins cross* down center *to table, carrying a basket of vegetables.*

TOM *begins to chop vegetables. The faucet drips very loudly. He goes to the faucet, turns it tight, watches it for a second. Satisfied, he returns to his chopping board. The dripping resumes. He goes to the faucet again, turns it, then takes out a metal pail. He sits on it and pees. Goes to the faucet, wets his hand and cleans under his slip, then dries with a hair dryer. He goes back to the table, the drip resumes, and* TOM *begins savagely chopping a zucchini.*

JULIANA *takes a big pipe wrench from under the bed, crosses to the faucet, and pounds on it with the wrench. There is a moment's peace, but then the dripping resumes.*

TOM *hurls eggs into a mixing bowl, still in their shells. A stagehand wearing a black welder's helmet enters* stage right, *carrying a stool with a kitchen blender.* TOM *crosses, pours the eggs into the blender and whips them.* JULIANA *crosses with the wrench and hammers on the faucet again.*

51

TOM *puts the eggs in a bowl, then takes the table off. He pours contents of bowls into a pot and stirs.*

JULIANA *tears the paper from the typewriter. She puts the typewriter away under the bed, and takes out an old vacuum tube radio. She pushes the radio along the floor for a few feet, then switches it on. We hear the sounds of a horse race. Suddenly, a man's voice breaks in. They listen for a moment, then static overwhelms the voice.* JULIANA *quickly shuts off the radio.*
A video image of BORRACHA *knocking at the window appears.*

TOM: Go away, I told you before, we don't want any cookies.

*(*TOM *puts food into the dishes, then takes the buckets, utensils, etc., offstage.* JULIANA *sits downstage, takes out a pitch pipe. She plays a note on it, then sings part of an unrelated scale. Repeat. In the video image,* BORRACHA *bangs on the window again.)*

TOM: GO AWAY!

TOM *serves the food. He blows on his bowl then begins to eat.* JULIANA *sees that there is nothing in the bowls, pours her "food" on the ground, and bangs on her bowl with the spoon.* TOM *grabs her bowl, crosses* upstage right, *and hurls the bowl out the door. We hear a loud crash as the bowl breaks.* TOM *crosses back* downstage, *picks up his bowl.* JULIANA *blows on the pitch pipe and sings.* TOM *crosses upstage right, to the faucet. The kettle boils,* TOM *grabs it and burns his hand.* JULIANA *rushes over, takes his hand, kisses it, and lays her face on it.* TOM *raises her face to his, but as they are about to kiss, they hear loud sounds next door. Through the following, to* ALAN'*s voice breaking in,* TOM *and* JULIANA *listen, he with growing interest, and* JULIANA *with alarm. At the sound of* ALAN'*s voice, they both become fearful and bewildered.*

WOMAN: Fuck me.

MAN: No, I can't do that.

WOMAN: Fuck me now.

MAN: What do you want to do, get me in trouble?

WOMAN: Fuck me now.

Orgasmic noises

ALAN From the egg laid by night, say the birds, came Eros. We will cure you of your perversions. You return to your dung as a dog to its vomit. Come on, boys, throw her out the window.

(A crash. A scream)

Lights out!

The lights bump out.

The Bickersons—Dialogue I

JULIANA *snores.* BORRACHA *on video opens window, looks through, then disappears.*

TOM: Tommy, Tommy! *(Throws a glass of water in* JULIANA's *face. Sound of splash.)* Are you in pain?

JULIANA: Are you in pain?

TOM: What's the matter with you?

JULIANA: What's the matter with you?

TOM: Stop repeating everything I say like a parrot. Why do you repeat everything?

JULIANA: You just said that.

TOM: I know I did.

JULIANA: Well, why do you repeat everything? You are repeating like a parrot.

TOM: Very funny. I bet you're a riot with those broken down friends of yours. I never want to see them or your boss in this house again.

JULIANA: None of my friends have ever been in this house.

TOM: Why are you ashamed of me?

JULIANA: I'm not ashamed of you.

TOM: Then why don't you invite them here. Because they're a bunch of bums.

JULIANA: THEY'RE NOT BUMS! *(Knocks* TOM *out of bed.)*

BORRACHA *enters and begins to sing.*

TOM: Oh I just love that Xavier Cougat.

JULIANA: BUZZ-Z-Z-Z

TOM: Don't do that! When we got married I gave up all my girlfriends. Why don't you do it?

JULIANA: All right I'll give up all your girlfriends.

TOM: Oh very funny. Oh I wish we could meet some nice people. Why don't you join the Elks Club?

AMEN *enters, starts saying "stop singing" in Portuguese.*

JULIANA: I will next week.

TOM: You say it but you don't do it. Why don't you join now? Go on get up and join the Elks Club.

JULIANA: Are you out of your mind? It's three o'clock in the morning.

TOM: It's only half past two.

JULIANA: Oh, why don't you let me sleep? You know I have to get up early.

TOM: I won't let you sleep because if you sleep you'll snore then you'll wake me and I'll wake you and we'll argue and I won't get any sleep.

JULIANA: I PROMISE I WON'T SNORE. *(Falls asleep and snores.)*

AMEN *and* BORRACHA *exit.*

TOM: You always snore, week in week out. On Monday you snore, on Tuesday you snore, on Wednesday you snore, on Thursday you snore . . . oh, what's the use. (JULIANA *begins to have convulsions.)* He's having that dream again. Tommy, Tommy. *(Throws a glass of water in his face.)*

JULIANA: Yes, dear?

TOM: You said you wouldn't snore.

JULIANA: What did you say, Dora Lee?

TOM: I didn't say *(A bell rings. The dripping resumes.)* anything.

JULIANA: Put a pan under it. I'll have a plumber in the morning.

TOM: I have indigestion. I've never been so sick in all my life.

JULIANA: I'm awake now. What's the matter?

TOM: I don't feel well, Tommy. Call the doctor.

JULIANA: You don't need the doctor. I'll handle it. Where does it hurt you?

TOM: Right here in the pit of my stomach, it's a shooting pain. *(*BOR-RACHA *enters wearing dog collar and chain; starts singing.)* Oh I just love that Xavier Cougat.

JULIANA: BUZZ-Z-Z-Z

TOM: Don't do that. It's a shooting pain, it comes about every five min-utes.

JULIANA: How long does it last?

TOM: At least a quarter of an hour.

JULIANA: How can it last a quarter of an hour if it comes every five minutes. Huh? Huh? Huh?

AMEN *enters wearing same, speaks.*

TOM: Don't yell at me; I'm sick. If I say the pain lasts a quarter of an hour then that's how long it lasts.

JULIANA: Okay.

TOM: Ow! I think it's that meal we ate at the Captain's. The fish disagreed with me.

JULIANA: IT WOULDN'T DARE DARE DARE DARE DARE.

TOM: I never want to eat there again. Every mouthful was poison. And the portions were so small.

JULIANA: Well you ate like you were condemned. *(The last word reverberates and echoes.)*

AMEN *and* BORRACHA *exit.*

TOM: Well you have to be polite when you go out to dinner. I wish we hadn't eaten anything at all. Oh, my God, I'm suffering so terrible. C-c-c-c-c-call the doctor.

JULIANA: Oh, you don't need a doctor! It's just indigestion. I know how to handle it. I'll fix you some h-h-h-hot ginger ale and oatmeal.

TOM: Hot ginger ale!

JULIANA: Make a new man out of you.

TOM: You treat me for indigestion and I'll probably die of liver trouble.

JULIANA: Listen, if I treat you for indigestion you'll die of indigestion. Now you want me to help you or not, hey? Hey? Hey?

TOM: Not if you are going to yell at me. *(Weeps.)* You wouldn't yell at Gloria Goosby if she got sick.

JULIANA: Now don't start with Gloria Goosby.

TOM: I saw the two of you at the dinner table playing footsie.

BORRACHA *enters, pantomimes singing.*

JULIANA: Footsies.

TOM: You were so flustered when she smirked at you, you couldn't eat.

JULIANA: I wasn't flustered.

TOM: Then why did you put gravy on your ice cream?

AMEN *enters, speaks.*

JULIANA: I always put gravy on my ice cream. I put gravy on anything and you know it.

AMEN *enters, speaks.*

TOM: A likely story. And the gown that woman was wearing. She ought to be arrested. I think she purposely swallowed that fish bone so you could stroke her back.

JULIANA: I didn't stroke her back, and I'd done that even if she hadn't swallowed the fish bone.

All laugh.

TOM: I don't know how Leo stands for it. Leo honey, how do you stand for it? He is such a wonderful man and Gloria is always playing sick around him just to get sympathy. *(JULIANA grunts.)* A lot you care what happens to me. *Every time Gloria gets a headache Leo hugs and kisses her and fawns over her. Why don't you do that for me?*

JULIANA: I'm never there when you have a headache.

TOM: Why don't you make a fuss over me?

JULIANA: Now listen, Dora Lee. You are not sick and you know it, know it . . . know it.

TOM: If you cared for me, if you cared for me, if you cared for me, you wouldn't leave me.

JULIANA: I'm not leaving you. I'm going out on business. I'll only be gone twenty-four hours.

TOM: Suppose a burglar breaks in the house and fuh-fuh-fuh-finds me?

JULIANA: It'll serve him right.

BORRACHA *sings and* AMEN *plays tambourine.* JULIANA *does a frenetic dance.* Black out.

Lights up *as* TOM *whistles* "My Buddy." JULIANA *lip-synchs his whistling.* TOM *crosses* downstage, *lies down, and goes into a yoga position with legs over his head and buttocks in the air. Sound of wolves howling.*

TOM: *(Fondling himself)* Fuck me.

JULIANA: Shh. I can't do that.

TOM: Fuck me now.

JULIANA: Shh. What do you want to do, get me in trouble?

TOM: Fuck me now.

JULIANA: Shut up! Shut up now!

TOM: Fuck me now.

JULIANA: *(Sings.)* I do not know with whom Aiden will sleep, but I do know that Fair Aiden will not sleep alone.

JULIANA: *begins to cross* down *to* TOM. *There is a loud buzzing sound, then big band music under* ALAN'S VOICE.

ALAN: *(Voice over)* From the egg laid by night, say the birds, came Eros. We will cure you of your perversions. You return to your dung as a dog to its vomit. Come on boys, throw her out the window.

ALAN *and* BORRACHA *and* AMEN *enter.*

TOM: Oh my God, I just pissed myself.

TOM *and* JULIANA *struggle but are caught by* BORRACHA *and* AMEN.

TOM: He's feeling feisty.

ALAN: Get the bitch out of here.

9 to 5: Part One

ALAN: Hey, hot stuff, grab your pad and pencil and get your buns in here.

JULIANA: Yes sir. Good morning.

ALAN: Hold it. Just hold it right there.

JULIANA: Something wrong?

ALAN: No, no nothing is wrong. I just want to check your bod. Turn around for a second. *(He whistles.)* Boy you have a nice ass frame. But you ought to get your pants cut a little tighter. You need to bring them up just a little in the crotch. I mean you got a nice package you might as well show it off.

JULIANA: Oh, Captain.

ALAN: Come over here I want you to take a memo. To all personnel . . . Boy that's a great cologne you're wearing Tommy.

JULIANA: Oh, thank you.

ALAN: Stuff's turning me on. What's it called?

JULIANA: Stud.

ALAN: STUD! *(Laughs.)* Well, it's very sexy. Only I don't like that tie you're wearing. What happened to the ones I gave you?

JULIANA: Well, nothing . . . I just . . .

ALAN: Take it off.

JULIANA: Excuse me?

ALAN: Take it off. I can't work with those stripes glaring out at me like that. And how about unbuttoning that shirt and coat. You need to loosen up. That's better. Now where were we?

JULIANA: Your memo.

ALAN: Oh yes . . . by the way I have a surprise for you here. *(Pulls out a huge strap-on dildo.)*

JULIANA: Aah! Captain, I'm a married man.

ALAN: Forget about your wife, Tommy. I mean you may be hers in the evening but you are my boy from 9 to 5. Have a look now. Isn't this pretty?

JULIANA: Yes, it's pretty. But you shouldn't be buying gifts for me, boss man.

ALAN: Captain. Call me Captain. Let me put it on you. *(Puts the dildo on* JULIANA.*)* Don't worry, it won't bite. If it bites we'll sue. Now that wasn't so bad was it?

JULIANA: No.

ALAN: I love your hair. It's so sexy. *(Stroking her bald head.)* Why don't we go over on the couch and I'll lock the door.

JULIANA: No.

ALAN: Oh, let's be friendly Tommy. You'll have to be a little more co-operative if you want to keep this job.

JULIANA: I'm not that kind of boy.

ALAN: Oh get off it. One little kiss.

JULIANA: No!

ALAN: What's it gonna hurt?

JULIANA: No! I won't.

ALAN: Tommy, you get back here. Tommy, I'm warning you, get back here.

JULIANA: No I won't.

ALAN: And he's out the shoot, ladies and gentlemen. He's out the shoot. Look at him. Now the Captain is gonna try and rope this one up *(ALAN lassos JULIANA.)* and he's already got him down. Ladies and gentlemen, let's see how long it takes to hog-tie this disobedient imp. *(Sound of a stopwatch ticking)* Five seconds, ladies and gentlemen, . . . just five seconds.

(Verdi's Requiem *plays.* ALAN *pulls* JULIANA *over to the bed and pushes her onto it. A statue with* TOM's *face is brought on* down right.*)*

Slide onto the table. A twilight sleep. We can cure you. Incisions are made in the hairline, tucking sutures down the crease at the ear to the upper neck. Using a crowbar, he breaks a bone in her leg and em-buggers her. We're going to bore desire right out of you.

ALAN *exits.* TOM *appears in a doorway, whistles "My Buddy." The head of the statue is sliced off with a swinging blade.* JULIANA *stands up on the bed, and* AMEN *sticks his head through the bed and makes a birdlike cry.*

Ronald Reagan and the Conceptual Auto Disaster

JULIANA: Today was like an old, worn out film being run off. Dim, jerky, flickering, full of cuts, with a plot I couldn't seize. *(A trumpet appears in the bed.)* Incidence of orgasms in fantasies of sexual intercourse with Ronald Reagan. Patients are provided with assembly kit photographs of sexual partners during intercourse. In each case, Reagan's face is superimposed upon the original partner. You want me to fuck him? Vaginal intercourse with Reagan proves uniformly disappointing, producing orgasm in two percent of subjects. I can't fuck him! The preferred mode of entry overwhelmingly proves to be rectal. Forgotten voices wait for the rain. Empty condom waits for the rain. A knife blade and silence. *(Falls asleep . . . trumpet disappears . . . bell rings.)* Where am I?

ALAN: Twelve. (ALAN *keeps repeating "Faster" under* JULIANA's *speech until he* exits *on the line "steals his insulin."*)

JULIANA: In an extreme twelve percent of cases, the simulated anus of postcolostomy surgery generated spontaneous orgasm in ninety-eight percent of penetrations. *(Harp appears from under bed.)* I can't pay my bills. Better to die. I close my eyes. The archangels applaud. Multiple-track cine films were constructed of Reagan in intercourse during: A) Campaign speeches. Shut up. B) Rear end auto collisions with one- and three-year-old model changes. Shut up. C) With rear end assemblies. Shut up. D) With Vietnamese child atrocity victims. Shut up. *(Falls asleep.)* Where am I? *(Harp disappears.)*

ALAN: For the price of a movie ticket . . .

JULIANA: You can spend a couple of hours with a sociopathic madman with a Robin Hood complex. Watch him order the killing of oh maybe seventy or eighty guys and rub out a few himself. Then finance a hospital for the poor in his neighborhood and show his affectionate side by fondling his lawyer's breasts in a subway train. Or meet a hollowed ex-boxer who, despite having the shuffle, stubble, and odor of someone living in a storm drain, manages an affair with a gorgeous widow who cuts him in on a lucrative kidnapping scheme. He's not such a bad guy, though. When the k-k-k-kid falls into a diabetic coma, he kills the doctor who once supported him and steals his insulin.

TOM: Am I neurotic because I want a nose job?

JULIANA: Yes, yes, yes.

TOM: Will it change my personality?

JULIANA: I don't know.

TOM: What if the surgeon removes too much?

JULIANA: Was your father an overbearing ass?

TOM: I have bags under my eyes. I'm forty years old. I'm married to a man twenty years younger than me. Tell me, am I neurotic for wanting a face lift?

JULIANA: Do you have dimmed vision?

TOM: No.

JULIANA: Do you have gastric distress?

TOM: Stop asking me questions.

JULIANA: Take me with you.

TOM: I can't.

JULIANA: BUZZ-Z-Z-Z

TOM: Don't do that. Where's my head?

JULIANA: There. Sound. *(She motions "cut" and crosses downstage.)* She's bi, I've got coke, you want to party? Are you going to answer me or not? Mr. Martin, I gather that your plan to remove the show to planet Venus has miscarried. Is that correct?

TOM: *(As Mr. Martin, on video)* Yeah, it looks that way. The entire film is clogged.

JULIANA: In that case, where will you go, when you go, if you go?

TOM: That's quite a problem. You see I'm on the undesirable list with every immigration department in the galaxy.

JULIANA: Use Tom Metzger's Nova number, 567-68-0515. *(Sound of police.)* Disrupt. Attack. Disappear.

TOM: *(Simultaneous with above)* Look away. Ignore. Forget.

ALAN *enters.*

JULIANA: *(To* ALAN.*)* What do I do?

ALAN: Push. Push. Push. Push. *(*JULIANA *climbs on the bed and pushes* AMEN*'s head down till it disappears.)* Good. Sing.

BORRACHA *and* AMEN *enter and do capoeira.* JULIANA *hides behind the bed, then bangs the bed against the floor.*

JULIANA: *(Sings.)* "I am sixteen going on seventeen / innocent as a rose. / Fellows I meet will tell me I'm sweet / and willingly I believe. / I need someone older and wiser / telling me what to do."

JULIANA *pulls bed* offstage. BORRACHA, AMEN, TOM *and* JULIANA *dance the* Metropolis Dance *as skyscrapers rolled* onstage. *Stagehand appears in doorway with small coffin, which* AMEN *carries* downstage.

JULIANA: *(To audience)* Tinkerbell, Tinkerbell, you're blushing, Tinkerbell, you're blushing . . .

ALAN *enters.*

ALAN: Forget that Tinkerbell crap and get over here. *(Places the torture helmet on* JULIANA's *head.)*

9 to 5: Part Two

ALAN *(To* BORRACHA*)* Play! *(*BORRACHA *begins playing conga drum as* AMEN *pounds on coffin with hammer. To* TOM*)* Hold it right there.

TOM: What?

ALAN: Turn around for a second.

TOM: Is something wrong—do I have something on my skirt?

ALAN: Nothing is wrong. As a matter of fact everything is very ripe.

TOM: So what do you want?

ALAN: Take a letter to Vernon Henshaw over at Metropolitan Mutual. Dear Vern, as you know, the chairman of the board of Consolidating Companies, Mr. Russell Timsworthy, spends most of his time in Brazil working on the jungle-clearing operation. My contact here . . . Dora Lee, yesterday I'm afraid I got a little carried away. I—I would just like to apologize to you.

TOM: Oh, don't you worry, Boss man.

ALAN: Captain . . . call me Captain.

TOM: I've been chased by swifter men than you and I ain't been caught yet, Captain. Shall we get back to the letter now?

ALAN: Yeah—um—well—um—could you just come over here for a minute. I have a little something for you. You know ever since I made that stupid mistake about the convention in San Francisco I . . .

TOM: Oh you didn't make a mistake, boss man. You see I'll just have to make sure the next time that I'm asked to go to work at a convention that there is a convention going on.

ALAN: And nothing happened anyway, so why don't we just forget the whole thing?

TOM: Fine.

ALAN: Dora Lee, you know you mean so much more to me than just a dumb secretary. So I bought you something. I picked it out myself. *(Pulls out a pair of fake, strap-on tits.)*

TOM: Well thank you. You didn't have to do that.

ALAN: I know I didn't have to do it. I couldn't resist. I took one look and it had Dora Lee written all over it. *(Puts the fake tits on* TOM.*)* I mean it was you. Well, what do you think?

TOM: Oh, thank you sir, they're very nice.

ALAN: It's really nothing. Dora Lee, I'm a very rich man. I've got a checkbook here in my pocket—you just say the word and you can write your own figure.

TOM: Oh, I could do that now, Boss—Captain. I can write your name better than you do.

ALAN: No, Dora Lee, I'm serious. Don't you understand I'm crazy about you. You're all I ever think about.

TOM: Captain, I've told you before, I am a married woman.

ALAN: And I'm a married man. That's what makes it so tasty. Let me sit on your face. Let me sit on your face. Let me sit on your face.

TOM: Oh, go sit on your own face. The exercise will do you good.

ALAN: You dried up old whore; we're going to set your clit on fire.

I Don't Need God.

TOM: I don't need God. I don't need God. *(Repeats this until he is shot.* BORRACHA *stands on* AMEN*'s shoulders.* ALAN *gets a gun from an* *opening in the wall and hands it to* TOM. TOM *shoots himself.* TOM, BORRACHA, *and* AMEN *fall down.)*

ALAN: *Raus!*

JULIANA: Where are you going? Where are you going? *(She repeats this throughout the following.* BORRACHA *and* AMEN *place* TOM *in an incinerator.* TOM *climbs out the other side of the incinerator and begins painting himself white.* AMEN *opens the incinerator and pulls out a charred skeleton.* BORRACHA *breaks off a bone of the skeleton and brings it to* ALAN.*)*

ALAN: *(Holding up the bone)* The fuel! *(He places the bone inside a blender and turns it on.* BORRACHA *brings him an oil can.* ALAN *pours the contents of the blender into the can.)*

JULIANA: Eurydice! *(Word reverberates.)*

TOM: What?

JULIANA: I'm scared.

TOM: No you're not.

JULIANA: What do I do?

TOM: The place that you rip open again and again, that heals, is God. I'll be waiting for you.

JULIANA: I love you. I love you. I love—

She is cut off by ALAN *to dance the* Heaven Dance. AMEN *cries.* BORRACHA *makes fun of him. The dance ends when* ALAN *drops* JULIANA *and exits. Wolves howl.* JULIANA *stands up slowly and sings the* Lament. BORRACHA *and* AMEN *do slow capoeira. The song ends.* TOM *enters dressed as the travel agent lady and screams. A motorcycle is brought on center stage.* BORRACHA *puts a motorcycle jacket on* JULIANA *and lies on the floor with his head on her feet.*

TOM: Going to hell, dear? Looking for the perfect travel package? At the tip of the Baja Peninsula lies a land of beginnings. Horseback riding over the desert bluffs or relaxing under a palaba. Windsurfing across the sea or scuba diving under it. Things go better with Coke, dear, right? Or so they say. Just try asking Roscoe "Fatty" Arbuckle and Virginia "Boom Boom" Rappe, the best-dressed girl in the movies, 1918. When driving in a strange city remember this: discourtesy to pedestrians can turn out to be manslaughter. First advice, that'll be a dime. *(To the audience)* That'll be a dime. Are we dealing with the English as a Second Language class here? That'll be a dime, one-tenth of a dollar. Fork it over. You—front row center—I saw you put that booger under your seat before the show. Booger, booger, booger, booger, right down front, I said it and I'm glad. Well, if your conscience gets the better of you, lay that dime right down on the edge of the stage—I'll be looking for it. If you dream of dying beneath the midnight sun, take only a few intimate, personal items with you as luggage, dear. Why load yourself down? Second advice, that will be a quarter.

JULIANA and TOM Like the pig who lay on a barrow dead, eyes closed, pink, white eyelashes, trotters stuck straight out behind.

TOM: Move him out boys. *(BORRACHA and AMEN pick JULIANA up on their shoulders, run a full circle of the stage then seat her on the motorcycle.)* Frankly I don't care if you threw this puppy out the window. Move—move—move—move. Here's a bonus travel tip, my dears. When traveling in strange lands, you should always carry a few assorted sweets about your person to distribute amongst the native youngsters. *(He throws candies into the audience.)* Otherwise there's no guarantee the little fuckers won't get you flat on your ass in some historic plaza and commence to rend and eat your flesh. Katharine Hepburn, *Suddenly Last Summer.** Now look here. Where you're going there's no tourist information, no American Express, no currency exchange, no post office, no telephone, no trains, no embassy, no budget travel, no medical assistance, no habla ingles, no kissing madam, no pissing sir, and for God's sake, no fucking in public.

*Editor's note: In the film of *Suddenly Last Summer,* it was in fact Elizabeth Taylor, not Katharine Hepburn, who witnessed the murder.

Twenty minutes of silence followed from Fatty's bedroom, broken by a piercing scream. *(Video image of a woman screaming.)*

ALAN: *(Appearing in doorway)* If you lose all your money, don't fret. The pay phones don't work! *(Exits.)*

TOM: Also, don't take all of the family jewels with you. Other than the ones you . . . carry between your legs! *(He grabs* JULIANA *'s crotch. She yells.)* Say, that's quite a cucumber you got there. Well! That still leaves Fatty Arbuckle in his hotel room, with Virginia "Boom Boom" Rappe in his room, Best-Dressed Girl in the Movies, 1918, who may, or may not, have a Coke bottle rammed up her twat. P-p-p-p-p-p-poor Fatty! He really got fucked! But not, as it turned out, by Virginia! Now remember. If you make every game a life and death proposition, you're gonna have problems. For one thing, you'll be dead a lot. *(To* AMEN, *who's been drumming.)* Why don't you shit-can the jungle atmosphere, honey, I can't hear myself think. *(*AMEN *stops. To* BORRACHA, *who's been doing capoeira and yelling in Portuguese)* Take a break, José.

BORRACHA: *(To* TOM*)* Puta!

TOM: *(To* JULIANA*)* Time to go, Sport. Will you write? Don't worry, I will never be far from the telephone. Here's your fuel. *(Pours fuel from can into motorcycle.)* Where's my dough? *(Pulls a wad of bills out of* JULIANA *'s pocket.)* Just remember. We're making a movie here, and you're . . . the star. *(Pause)* Where you're headed, there's a clock that never strikes. There's a hollow with a nest of white beasts. The paths are rough. The hillocks are covered with broom. This can only be the end of the world. *(Takes out ignition key.)* And I alone have the key to this savage sideshow. *(*TOM *turns on the motorcycle, exits laughing.)*

Music. BORRACHA *and* AMEN *enter and dance.* JULIANA *rides the motorcycle with a video image of the road behind her. The dance ends with a video image of a crash.* BORRACHA *and* AMEN *push* JULIANA *and the motorcycle off left as* ALAN *and* TOM *enter right.* ALAN *places torture helmet on* TOM. BORRACHA *reenters, stands and pants like a dog.* ALAN *pats* BORRACHA *'s head.*

Overture to Forest

As BORRACHA *and* AMEN *push* JULIANA *and the motorcycle* offstage
left, TOM *and* ALAN *enter from* stage right *and cross to their positions.*
BORRACHA *runs back to* TOM *and attaches the helmet to his head, then
crosses on his hands and feet to* ALAN *and pants like a dog under dialogue.
Trees flown in; image of forest on screen.*

ALAN: You're deaf. You're dumb. You're deaf. You're dumb.

ALAN, TOM, *and* JULIANA *'s next lines are said at the same time.*

ALAN: You're deaf. You're dumb. You're deaf. You're dumb. You're deaf.
You're dumb. You're deaf. You're dumb. You're blind. You're deaf.
You're dumb. You're blind. You're deaf. You're dumb. You're blind.
You're deaf. You're dumb. You're blind. You're deaf. You're dumb.
You're blind. I'll release black widows in your granny's outhouse.
What will you do?

TOM: I'm deaf. I'm dumb. I'm deaf. I'm dumb. I'm deaf. I'm dumb. I'm
deaf. I'm dumb. I'm deaf. I'm dumb. I'm deaf. I'm dumb. I'm blind.
I'm deaf. I'm dumb. I'm blind. I'm deaf. I'm dumb. I'm blind. I'm
deaf. I'm dumb. I'm blind. I'm deaf. I'm dumb. I'm blind. I will, I
will, I will.

JULIANA: *(From offstage)* No you're not. *(Repeated at five-second inter-
vals)*

ALAN: I'll release black widows in your granny's outhouse. What will
you do?

TOM: I will—I will—

ALAN: I'll put sulfuric acid in your Listerine. What will you do?

TOM: I will—I will—I will—

ALAN: You are safe here. No one can touch you. But safety is the most
dangerous of all conditions. Yes?

TOM: He's coming for me. I feel it in the pit of my stomach.

ALAN: He won't get anywhere. Let the dead bury the dead.

TOM: But mother, how the fuck is that possible?

ALAN: Don't be coarse. It's just a figure of speech.

JULIANA: *(Appearing half-dressed in armor at doorway)* Where was I?

TOM *and* ALAN *'s next lines are said at the same time.*

TOM: He's coming. He's coming.

ALAN: Dahling, you look like a bit of ancient Egyptian kitsch. Just say no.

JULIANA and TOM: No?

JULIANA: BUZZZZZZZ

TOM: Don't do that! My mother tried to kill me by poisoning me with arsenic because she wanted to collect the life insurance money.

ALAN You're joking.

TOM: No I'm not. Vampires only come out at night. But she didn't succeed. The doctors at the hospital discovered it and then I testified against her. That's the way it goes with evil and crime. You do it and then it comes back to you.

ALAN: Wo er sich versteckt?

TOM: I don't know.

ALAN: Wo er sich versteckt?

TOM: I don't KNOW!

ALAN *burns* TOM *with his cigar.*

ALAN: We're making a movie and you're the star!

TOM: You think you can buy talent and then throw it out when you've wrung it dry?

ALAN: It's important to make up for the things you fuck up.

TOM: He's coming for me, my studpuppy.

ALAN: Liebst du ihn noch?

TOM: I don't know.

ALAN: Liebst du ihn noch?

TOM: I don't know.

ALAN *burns* TOM *with his cigar.*

ALAN: *(Removes helmet from* TOM*'s head.) Raus! (Sings.)* "Nights are long since you went away. I think about you all through the day, my buddy, my buddy. Nobody quite so true. Miss your voice, the touch of your hand. Just long to know that you understand, my buddy, my buddy. Your buddy misses you."

ALAN *and* TOM *dance the* Heaven Dance. *Trees flown offstage.* ALAN *drops* TOM *and exits.* TOM *drags himself off.* JULIANA, *wearing full armor, is pushed in on a wooden boat. A huge blue cloth is stretched across the stage, then disappears as* BORRACHA *enters as the dragon.* JULIANA *slays* BORRACHA *the dragon.*

Interrogation

Rockets rolled onstage. One is rotated to reveal torture unit. TOM *climbs onto it.* JULIANA *removes her armor. Video of* JULIANA *undressing with cast members watching.* ALAN *enters and sits in a chair.* BORRACHA *and* AMEN, *wearing medieval dresses, play capoeira instruments.*

TOM: Ladies, are you fed up with salads instead of meals? Now you can find a heaven no man can touch. Tonight's my night for a miracle. Don't count your calories a moment longer, ladies, count your happinesses instead. He's coming for me, my studpuppy. Now you can twirl up a plateful of pasta, bury your mug in a bowl full of Häagen

Dazs, or just tap into what makes you high—high—high—hiya kids, hiya, hiya! Introducing the amazing new weight-loss program from Phyllis Schlafly. No lies, ladies. With Phyllis's amazing new program you can consume, dine, feast, feed, graze, nibble, snack, chomp, ingest, inhale, absorb, chew, nosh, gnaw, guzzle, masticate, pig out, gorge, gobble, and stuff your face. Tonight's my night for a miracle. Under the guidance of one of Phyllis's trained technicians, make a small incision in the soft part of your inner upper arm. Hiya kids, hiya, hiya! Let the blood and the fat flow. He's coming for me, my studpuppy. Under the guidance of one of Phyllis's trained technicians, make a small incision in the soft part of your inner upper thigh. Tonight's my night for a miracle. Now you'll be waist deep in pools of liquid flesh. Yuck. Step out, shower off, for the next step is to eat.

AMEN *speaks a line in Portuguese.* BORRACHA *answers in Portuguese.*

ALAN: Is that what they call a Mona Lisa smile?

JULIANA: I can't make decisions at all anymore.

ALAN: Is London Bridge falling down?

JULIANA: There will be no more war, there will only be weapons.

ALAN: What do you want?

JULIANA: My wife.

TOM: He's come.

ALAN: Do you love your country?

JULIANA: Is my ass worth that much to you?

ALAN: Fucking should be devoted to the business of procreation.

JULIANA: On the rack, pregnant, the woman, the hangman binds. Heart would fain, he racks her till break.

ALAN: Have you ever stolen any material—books, magazines, small amounts of cash, office supplies, etc. from your place of employment or college library? Explain.

JULIANA: I don't know how many people were in the bathroom with me.

ALAN: How about the other guy that was in there with him? Do you know him? Do you know you're condition is pretty serious, Martin? Can you hear me, Martin?

BORRACHA and AMEN: Yes.

ALAN: Can you hear me?

BORRACHA and AMEN: Yes.

TOM: The question of a fatally wounded man.

JULIANA: The dog soldiers are on line to assassinate the governor of South Dakota.

ALAN: Shut up.

JULIANA: Head it burned, over oil it poured, not confess.

ALAN: Shut up.

JULIANA: Sulfur, armpit burned, placed in her . . .

ALAN: How would you feel in an area that had no running water, toilet facilities, or where you would be forced to spend extended periods of time in a tent? Don't respond. Sit down.

JULIANA: Of course I do. That's why I'm here.

ALAN: Sit down. Take a load off your feet as they say . . . and unless my eyes deceive me you have quite a load.

JULIANA: Did you fart?

ALAN: Why of course, dahling. Do you think I always smell like this?

JULIANA: Never mind. I give up. . . . I'll do the dishes.

ALAN: I got up from the chair to greet Suzette.

JULIANA: Set up! (ALAN *fires rifle.*)

ALAN: I couldn't conceal my anxious expectancy.

JULIANA: Set up! (ALAN *fires rifle.*)

ALAN: It had been days since I'd seen her.

JULIANA: Set up! (ALAN *fires rifle.*)

ALAN: And my heart was conscious of the absence.

JULIANA: Set up! (ALAN *fires rifle.*)

ALAN: I waited at the door.

JULIANA: Set up! (ALAN *fires rifle.*)

ALAN: Did you say Egyptian gods?

BORRACHA and JULIANA and AMEN: Yes.

ALAN: Did she say Egyptian gods? What a coincidence.

JULIANA: What kind of coincidence?

ALAN: Oh, there's the nicest little man.

JULIANA and TOM: Where?

ALAN: Call me when you're ready to come home. I don't want you out in the junkyard tonight.

JULIANA: Don't worry, mother. Peter will be with me.

ALAN: The door opened and then Suzette appeared, radiant in her skin tight klemperer . . . whatever that means.

JULIANA: I blame myself all the time for my faults.

ALAN: Would you rather serve in the overt or covert capacity?

JULIANA: I blame myself for everything bad that happens.

ALAN: Did you ever lose your luggage?

JULIANA: I don't have any thoughts of killing myself.

ALAN: Do you want a shave and a haircut?

JULIANA: I have thoughts of killing myself, but I would not carry them out.

ALAN: Would you betray the trust of someone who has supplied you with valuable information?

JULIANA: I would like to kill myself.

ALAN: We're making a movie and you're the star!

JULIANA: I would like to kill myself if I had the chance.

ALAN: The police are with us. Are you thirsty?

JULIANA *and* TOM *speak at the same time.*

TOM: Yes I am. Yes I am. Yes I am.

JULIANA: Give this man a dozen. Overseer, overseer, give this man a dozen.

ALAN: Are you thirsty?

JULIANA: Tied, dropped suddenly from the ceiling, hands, hauled up . . . the hangman and his helpers went to lunch.

ALAN: Are you thirsty?

JULIANA: Mother told us not to play in the woods for the next few days and we obeyed her.

ALAN: Well, she was a foolish woman. A good quality water pistol filled with freshly squeezed lemon juice is the ticket. You shoot the felonious fur ball right in the eyes and it will soon stop the canine harassment.

JULIANA: Soft white male, age thirty-five, wants to play with black lady with large buttocks. Bi couples welcomed for Greek and French culture.

ALAN: There was a bit of nastiness last night, yes? I once shot a big nasty cur with the juice and he never bothered me again. Dead animals are so useful, don't you agree?

JULIANA: Why should fucking be devoted to the business of procreation?

ALAN: I've never believed in getting too intimate with the help.

JULIANA: But you have. But you have. But you have.

ALAN: What is the best type of agent? A) An adventurer (ALAN *lowers screw into* TOM —TOM *screams.*) B) A pacifist. (ALAN *raises screw—* TOM *screams.*) C) A combination of the adventurer-pacifist. (ALAN *lowers screw—*TOM *screams.*)

JULIANA: *(Pants for 20 seconds.)* What's an adventurer?

ALAN: The adventurer does it for thrills. Set up! (ALAN *places a pomegranate on* JULIANA*'s head, then shoots it off.*)

JULIANA: Imagine for a minute, Billy, that you're one of my toes.

ALAN: Do you take orders well?

JULIANA: That you're a part of me. That you're unhappy.

ALAN: Can you carry out a direct personal command from your superior if you disagree with it?

JULIANA: The place that you rip open again and again, that heals, is God.

ALAN: Have you ever lied about your name, occupation, salary, or place of residence?

JULIANA: The place that you rip open again and again, that heals, is God.

ALAN: Shut up.

JULIANA: The place that you rip open again and again, that heals, is God.

ALAN: Shut up.

JULIANA: It's okay to show a man getting his balls kicked on TV, but not okay to show him getting his balls stroked. What do you want from me?

ALAN: I want your snails, your snakes, your groundhogs, your weasels, your Japanese beetles. You can't desire her.

JULIANA: Many Englishmen feel that flogging is the only answer to the growing problem of the "teddyboys." Do you?

ALAN: I don't know. I'll think about that.

All laugh.

JULIANA: I'll take her.

ALAN: You can take her, but you can't fuck her, or else I'll leave you with a mess of pet maggots to raise.

JULIANA: I'll take her.

ALAN: You'll take her, but you can't desire to fuck her.

JULIANA: It's okay to show a man getting his balls kicked on TV, but not okay to show him getting his balls stroked.

ALAN: Right. Don't touch.

JULIANA: I will. The agency does not believe in letting you stagnate in one position throughout your Agency career. Your upward mobility in the Agency is limited only by your own ambitions. Over and out.

TOM: Tonight is my night for a miracle. He's coming for me, my studpuppy.

ALAN: Have a pomegranate. *(Tosses a pomegranate to* JULIANA.*)*

TOM: DON'T.

ALAN: EAT.

TOM: DON'T.

ALAN: EAT.

TOM: DON'T.

ALAN: EAT.

TOM: DON'T.

ALAN: EAT.

TOM: DON'T.

ALAN: EAT.

JULIANA: I'm thirsty. *(Eats.)*

TOM: Don't swallow the seeds!

ALAN *exits.* JULIANA *sees* TOM, *crosses to him. They embrace and lie down.* BORRACHA *and* AMEN *sing. End of song.* TOM *gets up off floor.* BORRACHA *and* AMEN *exit. A twelve-foot penis comes up out of floor.* TOM *turns and reaches for it.* ALAN *shoots it down.* JULIANA *sits up and screams.*

Alan's Final Solution

ALAN: One God. One Party.

TOM: I'm queer. I'm queer. I'm queer. What's it to you, you fat PIG! Hey. Hey. Hey. Ha. Ha.

JULIANA *staggers towards* ALAN, *pulls gun away from him, and exits.*

ALAN: Anyone want a shave and a haircut? A close shave. Anyone want a haircut? You! *(Crosses down into the house.)* Do you believe God will touch you? I want to avoid a face-lift. Does it make sense for me to do facial exercises like clenching my teeth and so on? One of the things about male Oriental whores—when you buy them, their body is yours to do whatever you want.

TOM: Tonight's my night for miracle . . . *(Continues under* ALAN's *monologue.)*

ALAN: Roger, she died three months ago. You showed me a copy of the death certificate. Don't you remember? This one was old enough to know the score and had been to the bar before. So we go in, we go in and have another beer. Where's my Blue Lady? Where's my Blue Lady? *(Goes to Blue Lady.)* Blue Lady, love's going to get you. Love's going to get you. Love's going to get you. Always be as well dressed as your circumstances will permit. THESE ARE THE ANSWERS. Remember these answers. Number 1) Mazda. Number 2) Citizen Kane. Number 3) Quantum mechanics. Number 4) Forty-eight pounds. Remember. I slip this guy another five and he's all smiles. Well I wasn't going to stand around looking like a freak. So I started undressing and ordered the kid—his name was Safi—to do the same. *(To* TOM, *who has stopped his ad-libs)* Why are you stopping? Don't stop. Don't stop. Go. Go. Go. Tonight you will be robbed of your

Rolex. You will crash your car. Your house has burned down. Your baby suffocates in its crib. The babysitter gets stoned. There will be an earthquake. Iraq has the atom bomb. The ceiling above you will collapse. The man next to you is going crazy. Your wife wishes to murder you.

JULIANA: Liar, liar, liar.

ALAN: You'll lose your job. Number 5) Islam. Number 6) The fatal flaw. Number 7) Wise Man. Number 8) Après moi le déluge. Remember. *(To Blue Lady)* I have a card in my pocket with something written on it, and I would like you to read it to me in a low, clear voice. *(He hands the Blue Lady the card.)*

AUDIENCE MEMBER: I'm a self-starter. I enjoy and am excited by producing.

ALAN: *(To Blue Lady)* We're making a movie and you're the star! You believe that? Busy young creatures, you don't have a chance. So we all get up and I order beers for me and my whore. I got my drink and took Safi over to a small table by the wall and had him start sucking. Judas is posing with the Bee Gees in a white leisure suit. No one could replace Andy Gibb. Ashes, whiskey, and tears.

TOM: Do you know "Mrs. Miller's Greatest Hits"? I miss you. Come and get me.

ALAN: I don't want him to go. My memory is failing. My bladder is weak. My arches are falling. My tonsils and adenoids are gone. My jawbone is rotting, and now my little boy wants to cast me away and leave me behind. I'll end up in a geriatric ward. I'll have to have enemas. I will be incontinent. There's a heart miracle taking place! You! Stand up, put your hand over your heart and call that a miracle. You! Lift up your head and call that a miracle. Tonight's my night for a miracle. . . .

TOM: Do your flower beds have barren or weed-choked areas? Do they lack color?

ALAN: Shut up. Chico, you're so groovy. About this same time a marine busted his nuts in this guy's ass. And one of the sailors got up on a table and told a kid to suck his cock. You! With the glasses . . . am I neurotic for wanting a face-lift? Remember these. Number 9) The Tower of London. Number 10) You could have had a V-8. Number 11) Dietrich Bonhoeffer. What if Noah had failed? *(Wolves howl.)* A lady may remove her gloves or not when partaking of supper. Guests do not bid their hostess good-bye; they quietly withdraw.

TOM: As you examine your personal landscape do you see anything else you don't like or would like improved?

ALAN: Shut up. Boy, I couldn't take no more. I started busting my nuts and Safi started sucking cum from my cock till I was weak. *(He sings.)* "Love, your magic spell is everywhere. Love, I saw you and I knew . . ."

They had this rice wine and I started drinking it. I got drunker than a coot. We are as driven to kill as we are to live and let live. Isn't that so? I heard that. I picked up the bottle and I smashed it on his face, he dropped to the floor. Everyone turned. No one said a word. Round and firm and fully packed, I crowned the Shenandoah Apple Queen. Men don't get smarter as they get older. They just lose their hair. Isn't that so? I heard that. *(To* TOM*)* Why are you stopping? Don't stop. Don't stop. Go. Go. Go. Healing is like ringing the dinner bell to lure sinners to salvation. Isn't that so. I heard that. Before you kill somebody, make sure he isn't well connected. Here lies old Fred. It's a pity he's dead . . . I am obsessed with the little toe on my left foot. It is turning into a claw. A species that is going nowhere. And I'm having to do this alone. Not like Cousteau with his assiduous team aboard the sun-flooded schooner but here. Alone. Alone. Alone.

Question number 1) What is the name shared by the Zoroastrian Creator God of Light and a popular car? Question number 2) What film was consistently booed at the 1940 Academy Awards? Question number 3) What does the Heisenberg Uncertainty Principle apply to? Question number 4) What did Oprah Winfrey Lose? Question number 5) What is Arabic for submission to God's will? Question number 6) What did Louis XV never really say? Question number 7) Where were the little princes kept? Question number 8) Who said religion should take place in the marketplace of life? Question number 9) What is the phrase which illustrates the economic principle of opportunity cost?

You could have had a V-8. You fucked up. *(He chops off his finger. Scream begins and continues under* Ballroom Dance.*)* I'd like to cut off a dead man's member and have it sewn onto me. I should like to be a man. I should like to rob a dead man's soul before it went to heaven and turn myself into a man. I would then seduce all women. I want to taste every man and every girl. I believe you are too good for this calling. I'd like to wallow in something, just so that I can say I've wallowed in it. I know it now. I'd like to wallow in corpses. I want to be stronger and stronger. I have never had a facial injury. I think I'd go mad if I ever did. Is my body now obsolete? Is my body now obsolete? Is my body now obsolete? *(A tiny casket is lowered.* ALAN *opens the casket and the sound of the scream moves into it. He turns and throws the casket towards the video screen. Video image of a casket crashing through a window.* Blackout.*)*

BORRACHA *and* AMEN *dance with machetes in semi-darkness.* JULIANA *opens upstage door and leans through.*

JULIANA: *(Whispering at door)* Go and wash yourself, I'm coming to get you. *(Repeats until stage* lights *are brought up, then closes door.* ALAN crosses upstage *to door and bangs on it.)*

ALAN Öffnen die Tür. *(He repeats this ten times.)*

The entire back wall collapses. JULIANA *is revealed as the Blue Angel carrying a sword.* ALAN *and* JULIANA *walk slowly* downstage. JULIANA *stabs* ALAN. BORRACHA *and* AMEN *embrace.* TOM *crawls out of a trap door.* ALAN *dies. A blue curtain slowly closes.*

While the blue curtain remains closed, a Wonder Woman radio show is played. BORRACHA *comes through the curtain carrying a tray of cookies and condoms. He throws cookies and condoms into the audience, then exits through the curtain. The curtain is drawn revealing* TOM *and* JULIANA *posed in a pastoral scene.*

TOM: Darling, I thought that fat slob would never shut up.

JULIANA: I want to be alone with you forever. My application to enter the United States has arrived.

TOM: Wonderful! Hurry and fill it out. I'll help you.

They dance downstage *saying "Am I right?" "You are wrong." "Are you wrong?" "Right I am." etc., until they reach their next position.*

TOM: Oh, if I had to sail for home without you, I'd just shoot myself.

JULIANA: No, you wouldn't.

TOM: You're right, I probably wouldn't.

They dance across right, *again alternating the lines "Am I right?" "You are wrong," etc., until they reach the next position.*

TOM: Darling, was it bad?

JULIANA: I'd rather not talk about that.

TOM: Whatever you say.

They dance to center *repeating "Am I right," "Am I wrong" sequence.*

JULIANA: You're a trusting soul, aren't you?

TOM: You didn't kiss me good night.

JULIANA: I am you.

TOM: You I am.

JULIANA: Wanderers cling to their fading homes.

TOM: *(As they break away and move* downstage *doing a chorus line kick step)* You didn't kiss me good night!

JULIANA: What's red and sits in the corner?

TOM: What darling?

JULIANA: What's red and sits in the corner?

TOM: What darling.

JULIANA: *(As they meet in the middle)* A baby chewing on a razor blade.

An upside down tree flies in with a baby in its branches: Sound of a baby crying. TOM *walks towards it, sits down in lotus position.* JULIANA *falls asleep on the floor. Sound of snoring.*

TOM: Oh please, not that again, quit it!

JULIANA: *(Waking up, rising to her feet)* What is it?

TOM: There must be something that will put an end to that hideous snoring. Why do you do it?

JULIANA: Do what?

TOM: Snore. *(* JULIANA *turns and crosses to* TOM, *grabs his wrists.)* I'm going out of my mind *(* JULIANA *pulls* TOM *around;* BORRACHA *appears behind the window upstage.)* For years you've been telling people you have insomnia. Not only do you sleep like a log, but you sound like you're sawing it! The house could fall down and you'd never know it!

JULIANA: *(As she and* TOM *slide step away from each other)* Very funny.

TOM: It's not funny, it's tragic.

JULIANA: Say something nice.

TOM: I love you.

They run and embrace center.

JULIANA: The secret of flesh is in the lost Mayan books. All the forces of suppression have now converged on Mexico to find these books and prevent a new race of beings on this planet.

TOM: Darling, Ornament Magazine is here to take our picture. Smile. *(They smile. A flash. They press their heads together and turn left, right, and then a full circle. Sound of conga drums. They sink to the floor. Sound of knocking.* JULIANA *stands up and drags* TOM *slowly across the floor.)* Oh there's that boy again. I told him before we didn't want any cookies. *(To* BORRACHA *in the window)* Please go away. We don't want any cookies. *(*TOM *and* JULIANA *freeze for a moment. Then* JULIANA *crosses to the tree, detaches baby, and carries it upstage, reciting a Danish children's rhyme.* TOM *mimes rocking the baby.)*

TOM: Oh, the baby. Oh, the baby. Oh, the pretty baby. *(*TOM *crosses up to* JULIANA *and the baby, then goes offstage and returns with a papier-mâché turkey.)*

AMEN *enters dressed as a milkman, carrying bottles. Sound of Nat King Cole singing Christmas carols.*

TOM: *(To* AMEN*)* Merry Christmas, Mr. Howard.

AMEN: Thank you. *(Picks up empty bottles and leaves full ones).* Merry Christmas, Ma'am. *(Turns to leave but doesn't.)*

JULIANA: *hands the baby to* TOM *and crosses to get the milk. She comes back to the table, pours a glass of milk, and pulls a leg off the turkey and puts it on a plate. She takes the plate and glass to* BORRACHA, *who is still standing behind the window.* ALAN *shuffles on stage left, out of fatsuit and wearing dingy longjohns.* JULIANA *crosses to the lawnmower and begins to mow.*

ALAN: 1) At night I am woken up, bathed in sweat, by a cough which strangles me. My room is too small. It is full of archangels. 2) I know I have loved too much. I have stuffed too many bodies, used up too many orange skies. I ought to be stamped out. 3) The thin white bodies, the softest of them, have stolen my warmth, they went away from me fat. Now I'm thin and freezing. Many blankets are piled on top of me. I'm suffocating. 4) I suspect they will want to fumigate me with incense. My room is flooded with holy water. They say I have got Holy Water Dropsy. And that's fatal. 5) My sweethearts bring a bit of quicklime with them in hands which I have kissed. The bill comes for the orange skies, the bodies, and the rest. I cannot pay it. 6) Better to die. I lean back. I close my eyes. The archangels applaud.

During ALAN's *monologue,* JULIANA *stops mowing, crosses to the sink and washes compulsively. The faucet begins to drip.* TOM *and* JULIANA *kiss.* JULIANA *takes the baby from* TOM.

JULIANA: *(Singing to the baby)* Tinkerbell, Tinkerbell, back from hell, we wish you well. *(Spoken)* Little fat man, lick the pot man, tallest man, gilded man, little St. Peter the actor man. *(Wolves howl.* JULIANA *sings)* "Children of the Heavenly Father / safely in His bosom gather / nestling bird or star in Heaven / ne'er a refuge e'er was given.

Lights slowly fade.

THE END

The Hip-Hop Waltz of Eurydice, at the Los Angeles Theatre Center, 1990. Juliana Francis as Orpheus en route to hell in the "I Don't Need God" section. Photo: R. Kaufman.

The Hip-Hop Waltz of Eurydice, at the Los Angeles Theatre Center, 1990. Alan Mandell as the Captain, with Tom Fitzpatrick's Eurydice in the background, in the "Overture to Forest" section. "You are safe here. No one can touch you. But safety is the most dangerous of all conditions. Yes?" Photo: R. Kaufman.

The Hip-Hop Waltz of Eurydice, at Los Angeles Theatre Center,
1990. *Left to right:* Borracha, Juliana Francis, Alan Mandell, Tom
Fitzpatrick, Joselito Amen Santo, from "The Interrogation Scene":
"There will be no more war, there will only be weapons." Photo:
R. Kaufman.

The Hip-Hop Waltz of Eurydice, at Los Angeles Theatre Center,
1990. Juliana Francis's Orpheus and Tom Fitzpatrick's Eurydice
embrace just before "Alan's Final Solution." Photo: R. Kaufman.

The Hip-Hop Waltz of Eurydice, Los Angeles Theatre Center, 1990.
Left to right: Juliana Francis, Tom Fitzpatrick, Borracha, Alan
Mandell. The wolves howl and the Captain shivers as the lights
slowly fade. Photo: R. Kaufman.

Bogeyman, Los Angeles Theatre Center, 1991. *Left to right:* Peter Jacobs, Juliana Francis, C. Gerrod Harris, Tom Pearl. The brick facade, three stories tall with over a dozen windows, was gradually stripped away to allow a less hindered voyeuristic intrusion into the psychic life of the characters—and playwright. Photo: Jan Deen.

Bogeyman, Los Angeles Theatre Center, 1991. *Left,* Juliana Francis; *right:* C. Gerrod Harris (in upside-down bed), Tom Pearl (wearing horn), unidentified person on floor. "This must be a suicide planet." Photo: Jan Deen.

Bogeyman, Los Angeles Theatre Center, 1991. *Left to right, top to bottom:* Cliff Diller, Tony Torn, Tom Fitzpatrick, Juliana Francis, C. Gerrod Harris, Peter Jacobs, Steffan Santoro. Five of the nine discrete sections in the three-story set. Photo: Rosemary Kaul.

Bogeyman, Los Angeles Theatre Center, 1991. *Left to right:* Tom
Pearl, C. Gerrod Harris, Tom Fitzpatrick, Peter Jacobs. The end of
the play, featuring the death of the patriarch and the gay couple's
retreat to Mars. Photo: Rosemary Kaul.

The Law of Remains, at the Diplomat Hotel in New York City,
1992. *Left to right:* Juliana Francis, Steve Francis *(behind her),*
Tom Pearl as Jeffrey Dahmer. Photo: Paula Court.

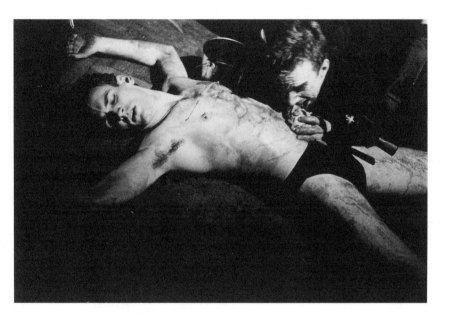

The Law of Remains, at the Diplomat Hotel in New York City, 1992. Brenden Doyle being devoured by Tom Pearl's Jeffrey Dahmer. Photo: Paula Court.

The Law of Remains, at the Diplomat Hotel in New York City, 1992. *Left to right:* Brenden Doyle, Sabrina Artel, Tony Torn, Peter Jacobs, Veronica Pawlowska, Ariel Herrera, Anita Durst, Charles Rosasco. The Connie Francis dance break in the section entitled "The White Room." Photo: Paula Court.

The Law of Remains, at the Diplomat Hotel in New York City, 1992. Rupert Skinner with unknown fencer *(face at center is a mask, not a person)*. White feathers and dollar bills fall as their duel takes place, near the end of the final section of the performance, called "Heaven." Photo: Paula Court.

Tight Right White, 440 Lafayette Street in New York City, 1993.
Tony Torn's Moishe Pipik stands over his mother, played by
Tom Fitzpatrick. Photo: Paula Court.

Tight Right White, 440 Lafayette Street in New York City, 1993.
Left to right: James Williams, Royston Scott, Randi Pannell.
Photo: Paula Court.

Tight Right White, 440 Lafayette Street in New York City, 1993.
Left to right: Royston Scott, Brenden Doyle, Tom Fitzpatrick.
Photo: Paula Court.

Quotations from a Ruined City, 448 W. 16th Street in New York City, 1994. *Left to right:* Peter Jacobs, Tom Pearl. Photo: Paula Court.

Quotations from a Ruined City, 448 W. 16th Street in New York City, 1994. Tom Fitzpatrick *(wielding plunger)* and Tony Torn. Photo: Paula Court.

Quotations from a Ruined City, 448 W. 16th Street in New York City, 1994. *Left to right:* Tom Pearl, Tom Fitzpatrick, Ken Roht, Brenden Doyle, Mel Herst, Sabrina Artel. Photo: Paula Court.

Quotations from a Ruined City, 448 W. 16th Street in New York
City, 1994. *Featured:* Mario Gardner. Photo: Paula Court.

Quotations from a Ruined City, L.A. Festival, Los Angeles, 1993.
Left to right: Mario Gardner, Anita Dorst, Tom Pearl, Ken Roht,
Brenden Doyle, John Yankee. Photo: Jan Deen.

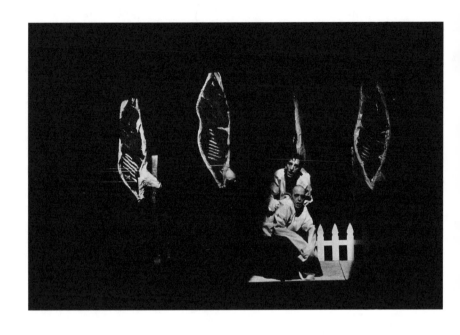

Quotations from a Ruined City, 448 W. 16th Street in New York
City, 1994. Tom Pearl *(above)* and Peter Jacobs. Photo: Paula Court.

Reza Abdoh. Photo: Joss Bachhofer.

III Reviews

Sylvie Drake

A Chaotic Plaint for Our Fouled Nest

Brecht said about Kafka that if you listen too hard you don't see. I wanted people to see.

—Reza Abdoh

A grim litany of facts comes over the loudspeakers in a steady drone as the audience files into the theater. It lists the dates of the first recorded natural disasters, the first human calamities, the first heart attack.

As the lights go down, a man with a shriveled arm limps on stage gazing unsmilingly at the audience. "Hi," he begins, dispassionately. "The law, Aristotle insisted, is reason free from passion. . . . " Then he outlines what this piece will try to be about, identifying himself as a lawyer who will also play a dead man. "It gets confusing," he concedes. "My job is to deconfuse," he says—and leaves.

The stage is bare now except for three axes, suspended in midair. Very still. Three people enter, seize the handles and start hacking—audibly—at the air. Three trees outlined on the back wall above them tilt with every blow. With the last one, they crash to the ground.

Is this the fall of civilization? The murder of hope? The end of life? How you interpret it is your own affair, but the image is memorable. So is the glut of images that follow—haunting, violent, graphically sexual, tender, pitiable, lyrical, humorous, and . . . confusing.

We were warned, of course.

It's a good thing creator/director Reza Abdoh won't explain his *Minamata* (though he will talk around it—in person and in the souvenir program). He shouldn't and probably couldn't. Not if what you want is reasonable explanation. This event is to be experienced—like Maguy

Originally published in the *Los Angeles Times*, May 14, 1989.

91

Marin's *Cinderella*, Robert Wilson's *Einstein on the Beach*, Tadeusz Kantor's *Wielopole, Wielopole*, or Richard Foreman's Ontological Hysterical Theatre.

For this and other reasons Abdoh's flight of theatrical impressionism at the Los Angeles Theatre Center (LATC) is causing a stir. It's the first spectacle of its kind and caliber to have been developed entirely in Los Angeles. It treats a subject that is always in the news yet rarely synthesized through art. And it compels attention by hurling images and sounds at its audience like an automatic tennis server gone berserk.

The script, dealing with ecological apocalypse, was written by Abdoh with Mira-Lani Oglesby (after he and his original partner, playwright Marlane Meyer, decided they were artistically too far apart to work together). But it's Abdoh's baby from there on out: he shaped and chiseled *Minamata*, with the help of his actors, designers, composers, musicians, and a choreographer.

The impulse for the piece was the tragedy at Minamata, a Japanese fishing village where a factory took up residence in the late '40s and began dumping mercury into the waters of the bay. First the fish became contaminated, then the cats who ate the fish, and finally the villagers and their children.

In Abdoh's piece, however, this industrial accident is merely the springboard for a wider indictment of man's cannibalism. "Our lives are a continuing succession of opportunities for survival," drones the text, while the evidence mounts that man continues to foul his nest and subvert his future. "Quietly, death becomes a commodity," we hear. Over and over.

Leitmotifs, counterpoint, and eclecticism are keys to Abdoh's staggering creation. Words are only one component of the language spoken here. Image, sound, mood, color, tone are the others.

Sequences quicken and tumble like events at a five-ring circus. They get harder to absorb as the spectacle gains momentum, whirring by, spoken or sung—always on more than one track, always to the accompaniment of an assortment of sound or music, always backed by odd and compelling projections: eyes that turn into eggs, eggs that crack to release yolks, hammers and nails swallowed by fish. A sense of unnatural doings.

With scarcely a transition, we go from corporate types in suits and ties moving in regimental formation to a comical cocktail party among four neurotics, to the simulated live birth of a full-grown naked man (the extraordinary Ken Roht) playing Alice, the deformed daughter of adoring, then despairing, then enraged, and finally murderous parents.

(Warning: This not a show for the squeamish or the easily embarrassed. It has everything from nudity to toilet scenes to simulated slashed throats and sex acts.)

"I'm interested in the physicality of ideas," says Abdoh. "The whole notion of decapitation, of castration, of severing one part of one's body or soul and still allowing it to flower—a phoenix from the ashes—interests me. History is loss. A baby is a loss of one's own flesh given to the larger universe."

So heads pop up from the floor. A corporate executive recites lame excuses for industrial abuses from an elevator-like box at the top of the proscenium. A bearded lady in top hat turns animals into skeletons. All the while, traditional and original music (some by Jim Berenholtz, some by Frederick Myrow) contrasts with the visuals.

Sometimes a lone cellist plays sweet, sorrowful strains at a corner of the stage. Sometimes a performer on electric guitar accompanies the singers. Always there is an insistent score that segues undeterred from the percussive sounds of an African Pygmy chant to "Tea for Two" or the theme of *The Beverly Hillbillies* sung in Japanese. The performance climaxes in a sonorous crescendo mass (by Myrow) that underscores the next-to-last scene of the piece much the way Samuel Barber's *Adagio for Strings* supported and enhanced the battle sequences in *Platoon.*

Fantastic. Excessive. Indulgent. And not. The major problem with *Minamata* at the moment is its plurality. Too much happens too fast or simultaneously. It is painted on too many emotional levels to be absorbed at one sitting. Rampant abundance keeps us from focusing. And while this kind of panoramic display can keep you fascinated, it doesn't always involve you.

The result: Seeing *Minamata* once is simply not enough. Either tickets should be validated twice, accommodating anyone who wishes to return, or the show must be rigorously edited. At two and one-quarter hours without intermission, the latter is the more practical idea.

But is it the better one?

It is only on second viewing that the show's beauty, communicated by osmosis rather than apprehension, begins to set in. Individual scenes and moments may remain elusive, but an oddly coherent and uplifting essence emanates from the whole. In time, it is the sum of the disparate parts that works. In time, we realize that, our own frustrations notwithstanding, this is a breakthrough for the artist.

"Reality can only be grasped indirectly," says the 25-year-old Abdoh, who was born in Iran and grew up in England and France and whose favorite language is Farsi. His mixed cultural background finds its way into his work, leaving open the possibility that the work has both the fascination and alienation of a less familiar (and more universal?) sensibility.

He tells us *Minamata* gestated for a year and was rehearsed for eleven weeks and that it could not have been done without the support system and budget of an institutional theater. This is Abdoh's second piece at LATC. The first was more traditional.

He staged two David Henry Hwang one-acts there in 1986: *As the Crow Flies* and *The Sound of a Voice.* In other locales he did a *King Oedipus* and Copí's *Eva Peron, Rusty Sat on a Hill One Dawn and Watched the Moon Go Down,* and *The Peep Show,* a flawed experiment written with Oglesby that took place in the different rooms of a motel —a real motel, not a set design.

Minamata is the first full-fledged, rigorously structured performance piece to emerge from his unrestricted (others call it unrestrained) talent—which doesn't keep him from showing up at every performance, still fashioning, still refining ("There is no other way for me to work but continuously").

Does he ever "jell" his pieces?

"Theater is so ephemeral that the whole idea of 'jelling' (finishing) is antithetical. I never satisfy myself. The task of artists is to constantly try to dissolve their own genres. If you don't, you won't know what's beyond the bridge."

With such intense preoccupation with image, can film be far behind? Film is voyeuristic. So is Abdoh. There's a television camera that descends from the grid in *Minamata,* focusing by turns on the audience and on the stage. It is "not so much a symbol as a sign of being observed," says Abdoh. "Everyone is always observing everyone else. It has that kind of pornographic angle. We are always looking through a keyhole."

Of the hammer and nails projected on the back wall he says: "A nail is always being put somewhere. A hammer always follows. We're always designated to perform certain functions. In my topography I see patterns of perpetual aggression."

Of the recurring images of eggs and eyes: "It's a way of restoring timelessness. Our history is a process of endless decay."

But there is hope. The piece ends on a pastoral tableau. "I can't completely succumb to the notion of paradise lost," says Abdoh. "No matter how much we are pulled into the vortex of solitude, it's our duty to search for [solutions], to not give up the quest."

And so renewal sets in. Its turbulence over, *Minamata* ends on a scene of considerable peace and beauty. The three trees cut down at the beginning are standing in the center of the village, righted again. It is night. Lights glow in the house. A train weaves down the track. A kid rides a bike, a swing is swinging, a windmill windmilling, snow snowing, a cello celling—and a pineapple sherbet moon above is very large, very bright, very full.

But it's not over until the bearded lady doffs her top hat—and bows.

. . .

Sylvie Drake

A Waltz on the Wild Side

Some theatrical pieces are like road maps. They show you exactly where you're going as you go. Others project you like a missile on a course you can tell little about. In such cases, it is usually best to let yourself go along for the ride and check out the map later. With any luck, it'll give you some idea of where you've been.

So it is with Reza Abdoh's *The Hip-Hop Waltz of Eurydice,* which opened Wednesday at the Los Angeles Theatre Center. A prerequisite is that you float along with the piece, not searching too deeply for meaning and especially not for logic. If you're game, if you're open to seeming and actual incoherence and chaos, if you can take nudity and strong, often raw, but almost always striking language and imagery, the completed journey will be staggering, if not always as illuminating as Abdoh might like. Many of his symbols, analogies, references, and cross-references remain private, caught in the undertow of his own River Styx—his brooding creative juices.

The pleasures (for some they will remain problems) are overwhelmingly visual. The characters are androgynous or aberrant. The acting and performing is superior. In the case of Alan Mandell as the puppet-master of this menacing underworld, a sleazy blimp with a face full of warts, it is exceptional. The video projections by Adam Soch are—as they should be—disturbing and remarkable.

Sets, costumes, makeup, sound, score, and choreography unite under Abdoh's unblinking eye to reflect his abstruse but insistently single-minded vision. There is a there there, and it is reached not through the mind but through the senses. Anyone who appreciated Abdoh's *Mina-*

Originally published in the *Los Angeles Times,* December 14, 1990.

mata at this theater last year will find *Hip-Hop* to be at once new and familiar territory.

And just as seductive and impenetrable. The legend of Orpheus and Eurydice is buried very deep within the folds of this performance piece. The program offers subdivisions that acknowledge the legend ("Orpheus's Nightmare," "Murder of Eurydice," "Passage through the Elysian Sea," "The Underworld"). But were it not for that, the title and the recurring tug of love and war between Tommy/Orpheus (Julia Mengers, also known as Juliana Francis) and Dora Lee/Eurydice (Tom Fitzpatrick)—the genders are intentionally reversed—it would remain unrecognizable. The Captain could be any boss, authority figure, prison warden, or tyrant.

Yet the events that unravel on Timian Alsaker's sullied set—a dreary, water-stained, high-ceilinged cell with a bed and what is by turns a window and a video screen—communicate effortless menace.

Props roll in and out or drop from the grid. They range from oversized phalluses to food and a motorcycle, from instruments of torture to musical instruments (including the staff and gourd, attributes of pilgrim saints).

By far the most compelling visions occur on video, however, from Orpheus/Tommy's frantic motorcycle race on a highway of death, to exploding Statues of Liberty, the decapitation of animals, the torture of people and political superimpositions that send potent anticensorship messages—including maggots that eat away at a portrait of Jesse Helms and a naked dancing male body attached to the head of President Bush.

Not for the faint of heart.

A program note suggests that *Hip-Hop* is the offshoot of an actual nightmare: "Abdoh visualized an Orwellian society in the 21st Century where sex is punished by death. He heard a monstrous vice cop scream at a married couple named Orpheus and Eurydice, 'We're gonna bore desire right out of you.'" This is now a line in the piece.

Among his influences are Rilke's *Sonnets to Orpheus,* the movie *Blood Feast,* Japanese kabuki, Brazilian capoeira (a martial dance), Jasper Johns, Marcel Duchamp, Francis Bacon, Virgil, Antonin Artaud, Bertolt Brecht, Jean Cocteau, and Karl and Groucho Marx. Eclectic hardly describes it. Unlisted but certainly also present is Hieronymous Bosch.

There is a waltz. There is paradox. God, by any definition, is prominently invoked and sometimes repudiated. A kind of holy irreverence permeates the language. A dragon, symbol of Satan, is slain. A line recurs: "The place we rip open again and again that always heals, that's God" (Rilke).

The final pastoral scene, intensely reminiscent of the one in "Minamata," exudes a disturbing kind of peace that slowly degenerates into an internal landscape of desolation, abandonment, and fear.

Puzzling, fragmented, hard-edged and brilliant as a diamond, *Hip-Hop* cannot be dismissed any more than *Minamata* could. It is enormously skillful. Yet for all its amorphous genius, it exacts more admiration than passion. Perhaps that is a reflection of the world we live in. Or will live in. To quote another influence, the futurist J. G. Ballard, "In a completely sane world, madness is the only freedom." Whatever *Hip-Hop* is, it does not easily let you go.

Charles Marowitz

Los Angeles in Review: *Bogeyman*

The recession is as nothing compared to the regression. The athleticism of American capitalism will no doubt rescue us from the catastrophes of the S&L scandals, the unemployment, and the general lurch towards lower standards of living. But from the regression, our irreversible descent into a more primitive state, there can be no salvation. The drug-addled, plague-ridden, crime-infested society that nightly reports the murders and atrocities of a civilization going down the tubes is the legacy that will make us pathetic to our twenty-first-century survivors, assuming there are any.

Reza Abdoh's *Bogeyman,* a *cri de coeur* cunningly disguised as a performance piece, now tearing up the boards of the Los Angeles Theater Center, takes nothing less than the phantasms of modern life as its subject. With AIDS as his subtext, and death as his pretext, Abdoh has looked hard and deep into his own terror and reproduced the lineaments of his own despair. He has found horrifying parallels between his own fragile mortality (he is HIV-positive) and the cruelty of a society that encourages a brutal psychopathology as a normal way of life.

The production's most apparent feature is rage, but it is not couched in the form of social protest. It is more like a painful reconstruction of the metaphysic that underlies all social injustice and nourishes all evil. Indeed, one is constantly reminded of Goya and Baudelaire: the former's obsession with clinically depicting human cruelty and the latter's descent into the living hell that everyday life is for *poetes maudit.* And if *Bogeyman* has a literary antecedent, it is unquestionably Antonin Artaud, who was the first to compare the theater's function to that of the plague.

Originally published in *TheaterWeek* 5, no. 10 (1991): 34–35.

"Like the plague," Artaud wrote, "the theater is a formidable call to forces that impel the mind by example to the source of conflicts. . . . The plague takes images that are dormant, a latent disorder, and suddenly extends them in the most extreme gestures. . . . In the true theater, a play disturbs the senses' repose, frees the repressed unconscious, incites a kind of virtual revolt . . . and imposes upon the assembled collectivity an attitude which is both difficult and heroic."

All of these observations apply majestically to *Bogeyman.*

From its opening Dantesque image—the exterior of a house that invites us to peer into the personal hells of ten tortured souls—to those Bosch-like tableaux in which sado-masochistic couples copulate, masturbate, have their genitals castrated by chain-saws, and are maniacally tortured by anonymous authorities as well as each other, the bleakness of Abdoh's vision is remorseless. But we should make no bones about it: this is a gay inferno, and Abdoh is glorying in the perversity as much as he is chronicling it. It is unsightly, ferocious, redundant, inexorable —a mirror image of the nightmare world that is both *Bogeyman*'s subject matter and its artists' natural habitat. Try as they may (and they barely try at all), the show's architects cannot shrug off the homoerotic exoticism that gives the evening a sense of special pleading. This is Charles Ludlam's world perceived by Genet and rendered by the Marquis de Sade.

There is a sign on the door of the theater giving clear warning of the nudity, so the audience members who leave during the performance are not responding merely to the sight of male and female genitalia. It is the relentlessness of the visual and aural obscenity that makes *Bogeyman* unbearable for certain segments of the audience—although it is those same features, this maniacal extremism, that take it into realms where neither Robert Wilson nor Richard Foreman has ever wandered.

The wildly assorted cast of characters includes a physically handicapped Fairy Godmother (Sandie Crisp); a tyrannical father figure (Tom Fitzpatrick) who epitomizes the totalitarian virtues of the bourgeois paterfamilias; his sexually neurotic spouse (Juliana Francis), costumed like Elsa Lanchester out of Bride of Frankenstein; and a number of carnal transvestites who weave wildly through the tapestry, performing assorted acts of fellatio and buggery. A collage of shrieked verbal fragments sets the aural tone throughout the piece. It is the hysterical sound of the desperate inner city—New York or L.A.—where the dissonance is so great that it drowns out all individual voices.

A vague thread of narrative concerning Billy, the Bugler Boy, and his peregrinations through an abusive family and corrupting world winds through the evening. But the story is as fragile as a cobweb and has no real impact on the imaginary events that are essentially the fabric of the piece.

Bogeyman consists of a series of arbitrary vignettes conjured up by Abdoh and based on a number of personal hallucinations. Where these connect with our own notions of universal angst, they register strongly. Where they don't, we watch them for their theatrical idiosyncrasy.

The multifarious setting is by Timian Alsaker and the costumes by Marianna Elliot. But essentially, everything we see is a figment of Abdoh's tortured imagination. It is very much a one-man Rorschach drawing.

As bas-relief, Abdoh provides a few moments of bourgeois serenity (a family picnic, a mundane baseball game) to drive home the point that no matter how much we upholster the facades, beneath them the nightmare rages unabated. Or to put it more directly: No matter how much we distract ourselves from the fact, the AIDS epidemic is an inescapable reality, and the superstitious desire to relegate it to one segment of the population cannot prevent us from stumbling over corpses or getting the stench of deadly tumescence into our nostrils.

What is fascinating about this piece is the unmitigated quality of Abdoh's inferno. It is unrelievedly savage. This is also its greatest weakness, for it occasionally has the quality of a child's tantrum—someone who is too busy railing against the injustices of life to combat them with artistic composure or rational intelligence. *Bogeyman* is a one-sided argument conducted by a whirling dervish whose spin is his rhetoric and who is too engrossed in condemning evil to work out a strategy to combat it.

The theatrical diction is postmodernist. It combines video imagery with frantic Artaudian writhings. Occasionally, it resorts to incongruous interpolations (hymns, pop songs, unexpected Latin American dance numbers) to disorient our expectations.

But whatever aesthetic quibbles one might raise about *Bogeyman*'s unfiltered dramaturgy or lack of variety, nothing can detract from its passion or its integrity. Producer Diane White is known to have personally bankrolled much of this production's expenses (it is lavish by LATC standards) and this may well be her greatest claim to managerial fame. If, as people suspect, this turns out to be one of the last croaks in LATC's swan song, it will have gone out in style.

Stephen Holden

Theatre in Review: *The Law of Remains*

The young Los Angeles director Reza Abdoh is notorious for theater pieces that have the decibel level of rock shows and apocalyptic imagery involving graphic sexual parody and violence. And in *The Law of Remains,* a multimedia extravaganza staged in the abandoned ballroom of the Hotel Diplomat, he has created one of the angriest theater pieces ever hurled at a New York audience.

A year and a half ago, Mr. Abdoh made his New York debut with *Father Was a Peculiar Man,* a spectacular theatrical deconstruction of *The Brothers Karamazov,* presented by the En Garde Arts company on the streets of Manhattan's meatpacking district.

In *The Law of Remains,* that feast has turned into a blood-soaked pageant of contemporary Grand Guignol depicting mass murder, sexual mutilation, necrophilia and cannibalism simulated by actors portraying the serial killer Jeffrey Dahmer (named Jeffrey Snarling in the script) and Andy Warhol and his entourage. The work is divided into seven scenes, scattered over two floors of the hotel, that are intended to trace the soul's journey as described in the Egyptian *Book of the Dead.*

The script incorporates lengthy excerpts from Milwaukee police reports of the Jeffrey Dahmer case. Focusing on Mr. Dahmer's beating and later murder of a teen-age Laotian boy and the casual response of the police who were called to the scene of the assault, it hammers home the point that because the victim was gay and could not speak English, the crime wasn't taken seriously and the boy was left with Mr. Dahmer. The event becomes a metaphor for governmental indifference to the AIDS crisis.

There is much to admire in the work, which is a skillful com-

Originally published in the *New York Times,* February 26, 1992.

pendium of avant-garde styles. The director's deployment of a fourteen-member cast suggests the grand ensemble choreography of Pina Bausch. His herding of the audience around the ballroom to witness a series of grotesque tableaux recalls Squat Theater. And the way the youthful cast is pushed to the limits of its physical endurance echoes the Flemish director Jan Fabre's *Power of Theatrical Madness.*

But *The Law of Remains* also continually undermines its own political ambitions. The sheer density of the noise and tumult make it hard to follow. And the notion of having Mr. Dahmer's grisly crimes re-enacted as a parody of a movie being made by Warhol and his fame-obsessed minions clouds the issue by seeming to attack the Warhol ethos for its kinkiness when the intended target is the mass media's sensationalistic exploitation of serial killers.

Never allowed to stay put for long, the audience is rudely prodded to move from place to place around the ballroom. This unceremonious treatment is only one aspect of a production that seems to want to punish as much as to enlighten. *The Law of Remains* is a disturbing work that runs amok in its own imagination.

Michael Feingold

Artaud You So

For the last hundred years, so much art has come out of the artist's taking an actively hostile stance toward the audience that you'd think we would all be inured to it by now. Yet it only takes an artist like Reza Abdoh, whose exceptional gifts include a truly exceptional violence of approach, to remind us sharply that the question modern art raises has never been fully answered, and the century is ending as it began, with artists and audience more unsure than ever about where they stand in relation to each other. *Tight Right White* is a piece of intense and revolting accomplishment, executed with enormous skill, that assaults audiences with a near-two-hour barrage of obscenely racist images, for purgative purposes: a psychological enema, shoved up the id of liberal theatergoers to expel the unhealthy imprints a racist society has deposited there.

This description isn't meant to encourage or avert potential ticket buyers, only to suggest possible larger justifications for a work that has, among its subsidiary intentions, the desire to arouse an almost continual flow of outrage. Whether Abdoh succeeds at this latter task is a question raising a whole separate set of issues. Obviously, every individual's reaction will be different; personally, I sat through the entire piece chiefly because I get paid to do so, secondarily because the setup makes walking out almost impossible. Despite my feeling that Abdoh has genius of a kind, I doubt that any newspaper could pay enough for me to endure it a second time.

The notion that theater could cleanse audiences spiritually by rattling them viscerally begins with Antonin Artaud, lunatic-in-chief of modern French literature, who posited a "Theater of Cruelty" that

Originally published in the *Village Voice* 38, no. 12 (1993): 93, 97.

would do away with anything that might keep spectators at a distance, bombarding them with words and images till they were in immediate contact with the reality at the core of the representation—not watching a play about Oedipus, say, but experiencing in their own body the reality behind the myth of Oedipus. Like other aspects of Artaud's thought, this one was prophetic: his slogans ("total theater," "no more masterpieces") have become bywords, his suggestions premises; the plays he seized on as alternatives to the stultifyingly familiar classics are part of the standard repertoire.

But the assimilation of Artaud's ideas by the mainstream has never actually meant their realization, for the very good reason that they are literally crazy; Artaud, who probably had a mild schizophrenia of the kind drugs can correct these days, was in and out of mental hospitals all his life. (He was a junkie, too, whose constant migraines drove him to opium and morphine.) In his fantasies, he created a theater so extreme that to make it real would set its audience wholly at odds with the outside world: having been transfigured by the vicarious experience of violence, they would be incapable of participating in or even imagining actual violence.

This contortedly idealistic view of human nature, reflecting the deep division in Artaud's personality, has clear links with totalitarianism, which was perpetrating elaborate theatrical rituals of its own at the time: Hitler liked total theater, too, for less pacific reasons. Artaud hated bloodshed—he was quick to point out that "Theater of Cruelty" didn't mean a mere wallowing in gore—but violence is at the core of his imagery, his language, his method. His work comes off as a constant flailing toward inner peace.

Tight Right White is what results when an artist of Abdoh's power filters Artaud's premises through the chaos of the 1990s. There are no seats; the audience is handed cushions and shuttled from area to area, though the unremitting action is the same whatever the space. The performance surrounds the spectators, its most elaborate scenes happening on either side of the main space while a marginal, commentary-like event goes on in front. "In this spectacle, sound effects are constant," wrote Artaud, and technology has made this particular dream instantly fulfillable, in Abdoh's case with a taped collage of rock, rap, Verdi, show tunes, and anything else that can be tossed into the mix for a high-decibel effect, plus live drums, likewise amplified to the eardrum-bursting max.

In keeping with Artaud's dethroning of text, the matrix of *Tight*

Right White is a ferocious, shredding burlesque of a work that was garbage to begin with—Richard Fleischer's repellent 1975 film version of Kyle Onstott's novel *Mandingo,* set on a Louisiana "slave-breeding plantation." A hashed redaction of its text is screamed out at looney-tunes top speed, its many acts of sex or violence done in graphic, grotesque form: cartoon lynchings, floggings, rapes, and even a disemboweling.

Stage center, a caricature Jew, in a fat suit and cartoon hooked nose, interviews over and over again a caricature street black, their dialogue including racist vaudeville routines and ethnic-slur jokes, anti-black, anti-Jewish, and anti-white. (There are also anti-Asian stereotypes and homophobic gags.) Video monitors above the stage, when not showing in live close-up the bare buttocks of actors being spanked in mime, display a tape collage of gunfights and explosions from action movies. The performers include blacks in whiteface, whites in blackface, blacks in blackface and a few whose heads or torsos are colored blood-red. The only relief from the barrage of vile talk and vile action comes in the form of dance sequences, ranging from minstrel-show versions of nineteenth-century ballroom dance through fairly menacing hip-hop jamborees to a stately Jewish *freilach.*

None of it makes sense, but then neither does racism, to accuse Abdoh of which would be patently absurd—though I suspect large numbers of African, Asian, Jewish, and gay Americans would fail to see anything in his work but a hideous outpouring of filth. The real questions are, does the work succeed in shaking our souls to the core, and, if so, is that in itself a good thing to do? I don't pretend to know the answers, though my general suspicion is that stirring up the muck in the id, and giving vivid external articulation to the ugliest myths buried there, while offering no perspective on them, can't be anything but counterproductive in the long run. People who pride themselves on their freedom from racist attitudes might be shaken by the discovery of a lingering unconscious prejudice; others are only likely to have their bigotries reinforced, choosing the hate they prefer from the many samples on display.

In this respect, the absence of any context from Abdoh's work is its most alarming element. Apart from the cartoon Southern plantation and its white-supremacist would-be heirs, no white world is visible; contemporary mainstream culture is represented by one stereotype Jew. There may be impoverished, urban African Americans who, in their anger, actually see the world this way, but Abdoh, who's of Iranian-

European ancestry, isn't one of them. *Tight Right White* has no link to the world outside, no acknowledgment that social and economic strictures are involved with the perpetuation of racism: only the perceptual matrix exists, a videocam eye, endlessly feeding recycled clichés into the glassy-eyed maw of the masses.

Artaud would probably be both proud and appalled. He loved the mental anarchy of America and spotted early both its destructive potential and its desire to pretend that the potential didn't exist. Abdoh apparently believes that rubbing our faces in the hidden hatreds as vehemently as possible is a step toward curing them. He certainly knows how to carry out the procedure; his is the most successfully Artaudian theater since the early days of John Vaccaro's Ridiculous. Those of us who lived through that earlier phase are entitled to be skeptical about the possible results: it's hard to imagine that unconstrained negative forces, once set loose, will provide any positive spiritual results. And if spiritual results are not the point, it's hard to see what all the negativity is for.

Elinor Fuchs

A Vision of Ruin

The woe and horror of history as ruination come pouring, choking, rasping out in the disconnected fragments of Reza Abdoh's *Quotations from a Ruined City.* "Sarajevo!" it screams. "Beirut!" And now Los Angeles, and now the concentration camps, the world as camp. Above all, AIDS, the organizing "metaphor." Or so a theater critic might say. But this latest work by Abdoh, his seventh major large-cast theater piece, can't be politely distanced as a "show," and it is pointless to fuss over its awkward and verbose form. *Quotations from a Ruined City* is an urgent personal testament: it wants witnesses, not spectators.

Reza Abdoh is the Iranian-born, just turned 30-year-old director—relocated from Los Angeles, which loved him, to New York, which has ignored him—of whose raucous, violent, scatological, aggressively homoerotic, and often elegiac theater pieces—performed in industrial lofts, derelict hotels, or the 14th Street meatpacking district—you may have distantly caught word. As early as the age of 20, doing a four-hour *King Lear* in a Los Angeles loft, Abdoh gazed intently at death. Death presided over the *Hip-Hop Waltz of Eurydice,* an extravagant Orphic descent into the underworld of future-shock authoritarianism. It sickeningly pervaded *Law of Remains,* Abdoh's vision of an interlocking show-biz-sadism directorate symbolized by an Andy Warhol–Jeffrey Dahmer collaboration. But now Abdoh is seriously ill with AIDS, and in the very personal vision of *Quotations,* the reign of death is absolute. Walter Benjamin's reflection—"everything about history that . . . has been untimely, sorrowful, unsuccessful, is expressed in a death's head. . . .

Originally published in the *Village Voice* 39, no. 11 (1994): 91–92.

The greater the significance, the greater the subjection to death"—could be inscribed over Abdoh's harsh and dolorous stage.

So AIDS is no mere "metaphor" here, and more than subject. Dying of AIDS is the very architecture of the performance, which reels from graveyard to oxygen mask to the sound of gasping for breath to coffins to funeral and *da capo* to graveyard to hospital, with the central sufferers each time a little weaker, a little more transparent. In between come brief remissions: feverish dances and love scenes. The torrential repetitions—throwing the actors into one more dance, one more speech, bringing on one more image, one more idea and geopolitical association—represent perhaps the most heartbreaking mimicry of the attempt to stay alive in the losing struggle with AIDS. So little in this piece suggests looking forward with hope that the removal in the final scene of the barbed wire stretched across the front of the stage seems gratuitously regenerative.

The cast of eleven represent not only the human ruins but the runners. These Abdoh concentrates in the figures of two white males, at first seen as ruffed and hatted Puritans, but eventually as black-suited funeral directors–financiers. Another Puritan, this time a woman, swings a murderous axe against the presumably Muslim enemies of the "Chetniks." Since gender-free casting is sometimes Abdoh's method, but sometimes assertively not, this is a troubling figure—especially given the infernal torments reserved for women in the Bosnian war. She later appears wielding a hammer, a knife, and a submachine gun.

One can find in Abdoh's work the idiom of the conceptual avant-garde of the past twenty years, but transformed through popular films, music, and dance. What Abdoh, more than any such "mentor" figure (Foreman, Breuer, Wilson, and LeCompte) brings to the work, however, is a sense of history. His performance piece of a year ago, *Tight Right White,* was astonishing in its vision of American racism/homophobia as a single, faceted construct handed on in every reshaped patrimony from slavery to the age of AIDS. The shattering energy of that piece, shouted and danced at frantic speed over five stage areas to a text largely composed of low jokes from the blackface and vaudeville circuit, is not duplicated here. By contrast, *Quotations* concentrates its forces, invests more in text, less in physical motion. But the vivid sense of historical linkage remains. I take Abdoh's threnody for Sarajevo seriously. As a Western artist from the Middle East, he grasps better than most Americans the tragic fault line of national identity that demagoguery turned into the Bosnian holocaust. All themes in Abdoh's vision of ruin, both personal and historical, come together in a horrendous account, only partly based on fact, of the live skewering of the "Bosnian Muslim Mustafa." The unseen Mustafa figures as sadistic sexual fantasy, raw meat, *anus mundi,* lamb of God.

Unlike any Abdoh piece I've seen, this one is almost replete with text, some of it quite powerful, some of it clunky-poetic or dialogue set pieces that lack the ring of theatrical life. Abdoh's gifted company lip-synchs almost all of this, but seems weighted down with words. The text, which threads together, *inter alia,* the narratives of two male couples, one powerful and indifferent, the other weak and ill, is Abdoh's first collaboration with his younger brother, Salar Abdoh. The piece needs distillation, which will perhaps still be possible because of its extended life in Europe. With presentations since 1992 in Paris, Barcelona, Frankfurt, Vienna, and elsewhere, international support has become crucial to the survival of Abdoh's theater. It is by now a familiar story that his immense L.A. works can find their way more easily to Paris than New York, or that his most brilliantly integrated piece in New York (*Tight Right White*) will tour abroad but couldn't get a *Times* critic to attend.

"Mankind needs silence and warmth, and we give him an icy pandemonium," Simone Weil writes. In every Abdoh piece I have seen, pandemonium gives way to a nostalgia for a lost pastoral, and an intense longing for the spiritual. This was his theme at the end of *Father Was a Peculiar Man* (Abdoh's adaptation of *The Brothers Karamazov,* which played in the streets of the wholesale meat district four years ago), of the heavenly epilogue to *Law of Remains,* and of the silent conclusion to *Tight Right White.* The pastoral note is heard only at brief moments in *Quotations.* Birdsong succumbs to urban traffic sounds and then to sniper fire. The graveyard transforms into a field of sheep before turning once more into a battle or torture zone. The final images of the play pit love and longing against the smug oblivion of a chorus line of uniformed Boy Scouts, but upstage behind this contest appear sides of beef on butcher hooks. Among the ruins of the ruined city, one may have to count redemption.

IV Essays

Gautam Dasgupta

Body/Politic:

The Ecstasies of Reza Abdoh

In a decade and a half, his biological half-life, playwright, director, and filmmaker Reza Abdoh has, with a potency unequaled in recent times, let loose a torrent of theatrical energy evocative of Armageddon. A maniacal (some might say, demoniacal) spirit guides his actors' actions on stage. Whatever the putative subject matter of the plays, the sclerous bodies of the actors, conspicuously magnified by the brutal application of epidermal scoriae (in varying hues and tonalities), leathery accoutrements, and severe fright wigs, bounce, flail, thrash, and charge across the stage in frenzied bacchanalian rhythm, a choreographed mayhem that is as unsettling as it is deliberate. Ear-splitting sounds, heavily amplified music, and the miked grunts, groans, and sighs of these denizens of another world, a netherworld perhaps, punctuate a narrative that is itself fractured by multiple and overlaid texts. Add to this mélange multimedia technology, television monitors, excessively detailed and cluttered stage sets vying for attention, and an ambulatory theatrical experience with audience members herded into separate areas, and one gets a fairly general sense of what it is like to be present at a Reza Abdoh–Dar A Luz production.

To be present is to do so at one's peril. There is much at stake here, as Abdoh's nightmarish and, at times, diabolical visions unfurl with mounting intensity before our eyes. Not for the faint of heart his gruesome depictions of mutilated bodies and sundered genitals, gory intimations of cannibalism and physical torture, and the vivid display of tormented individuals writhing in pain and crying out for release and redemption. In this marriage of heaven and hell, we are forced to contemplate in all its sacred terror a Boschian landscape, to bear witness to

Originally published in *Performing Arts Journal,* no. 48 (1994): 19–27.

113

the evils that surmount us on all sides. And yet, despite searing images of unrelieved horror, there emerges a glimmer, not of hope, but of courage, at having faced down or faced up to the monstrosity that we are all capable of inflicting upon one another. There is not catharsis, no purgation, in Abdoh's worldview, firmly situated and framed within a Manichean universe. Good and evil coexist externally, although good, for now, seems to be in retreat against the overwhelming forces of evil. Evil, in Abdoh's cosmos, however, is not a moral principle, but a life-denying attribute. It is a negative axiom that enters the world through social, political, and cultural denigration, and the abuse of power. It afflicts not only social relations among classes, races, genders, and diverse cultures, but, worst of all, denudes the body and the self of vital sources of nourishment. Not that I wish to underplay the social forces that activate Abdoh's dramatic instincts (the exploration of racism in *Tight Right White,* the brutal examination of the psychic manifestation of violence and the media in *The Law of Remains*), but what remains, for me at least, are the haunting images of shattered bodies entombed in their own private nightmares, of bodies in pain.

To do justice to Abdoh's theatrical visions is a daunting task. His prodigality is such that all attempts to render the complex vision that unfolds before one's eyes perforce minimize the impact of their theatricalness, their overpowering presentness and immediacy. The rapid-fire succession of images, the relentless compounding of theatrical metaphors that motor his pieces do not make for easy transcription onto the page. But even if that were possible, something would still inevitably be lost in the translation. What Abdoh's theater gives us is, in a sense, unwritable, or unspeakable, for it is, paradoxically, the ones unspoken for, those without a language, who are given a voice in his work. And these voices, unheard of within the dominant social framework or, when audible, painfully attenuated within the prevailing social, political, economic, and linguistic construct, seek out new models of being in the world or in a culture from which they are alienated.

It comes as no surprise that early on in his career, when Abdoh was nineteen, he directed *King Lear,* a tale as much about patriarchy and domination as it is about Cordelia's silence, a voice muted for not echoing the call of acceptable norms of social behavior. But whereas Lear's daughter had only the means of language to deny language's hypocrisy to express her innermost convictions, the characters in Abdoh's universe have access to a multiplicity of languages, mediated and unmediated—

private self and public persona, body and mind, gesture and voice, image and narration, the vocabulary of "high" and "low" culture, text, context, and subtext. It is the interweaving of these multiplicities, these shifting perspectives, that form the foundation of Abdoh's dense theatrology, his scenic forays into the social and political landscape of our times. If Babel this be, then it is so in the truest historical sense of that tower in the land of Shinar constructed with the purpose of reaching heaven.

But Babelism is as much a fact of ancient history as it is a fact of contemporary cultures, with millions on the move all over the planet. It is, and has been, particularly true of the American experience from its very inception. And more interestingly, perhaps, in America there has traditionally been a lack of centripetal notion of culture. Different races and different cultures have somehow managed to create their own models, be they cultural, artistic, or political, models that defy or undermine or stand in opposition to what appears on the surface to be a fairly uniform and homogeneous social structure. It is at these boundaries, these strategic sites of contest and struggle and conflicting voices where Abdoh places his artistry.

His personal history well equips him for this role as keeper of the gates. Born of Iranian and Italian parents, having lived through the turmoil of the Shah's reign and of the Ayatollah's messianic vengeance, he first found a home in Los Angeles (he immigrated to America at the age of 19 and now lives in New York), the land of diverse cultures and of seismic shifts, where cracks appear on the face of the land, reinscribing geographical fissures with as much regularity as each new wave of immigrant groups and cultures rewrites the social and cultural landscape of California. It is the uncongealed, invisible matter deep down in the bowels of the earth that serves as apt metaphor for Abdoh's theater, generated as it is by forces that are there, lying dormant or purposefully unrecognized, but forces that have the power to shake up the body politic in sudden spasmodic eruptions.

While it is true that Abdoh's exilic state has granted him new and varying insights into the social problems that plague America, the multiplicity of perspectives that he brings to his work encompasses more than just analyses of contemporary issues. Questions of identity (at age 14, when such issues were paramount in his thoughts, he directed *Peer Gynt*) and reflections on the nature of home and country (*Tight Right White*), the environment (*Minamata*), familial relations (*Father Was a*

Peculiar Man), and power, his grand subject, with its attendant attributes of death, destruction, and decay (*The Hip-Hop Waltz of Eurydice, Bogeyman, The Law of Remains*), are forcefully and provocatively posed. In all instances, personal displacements and struggles with identity, religious faith, ethnicity, homeland, and sexuality are reflected upon form within and in contradistinction to a broader social and ideological spectrum. A true rebel at heart, Abdoh is not one to search after fixed identities, refusing to take comfort in their regressive and reductive natures. In wishing to be born anew at each instant, and with each work, he employs relentlessly shifting perspectives, bringing into play a voracious appetite that engages multifarious themes, diverse cultures, social and personal histories (of himself, of his actors, of even the spaces in which he chooses to perform), past, present, and future, and, finally, the *modus operandi* of his unique theatrical style, which ranges from vaudeville to lazzi to cabaret to Borscht Belt to Bombay film musicals to Ta'ziyeh to puppetry to dance to technological media. If there is a true multicultural artist at work in America today, accepting the idea of the multicultural in its most expansive definition, then surely Abdoh is that artist.

It is perhaps easy to misconstrue Abdoh's theatrical temperament as a hodgepodge of styles, either in the manner of MTV or the pastiche-ridden and borrowed metaphors employed by the likes of filmmaker Quentin Tarantino (*Pulp Fiction*), playwright-director Tony Kushner (*Angels in America*), or the incestuous schools of simple-minded multiculturalism and vapid "postmodernity" that are addressed by artists and institutions alike from coast to coast. Soaring high above them, Abdoh's use of quotations, clichés, fragments are linked philosophically to his larger agenda, and not as mere decoration or artifact. In the fragments reside the stilled voices on whose behalf Abdoh has chosen to speak.

The title of his work *The Law of Remains* offers a clue in this regard. Fragments are what remain when the rest of the body politic of a culture or a civilization has been appropriated or consumed. They are the precipitate, the residue of all values that fail to enter the mainstream, shards of history that lie deep buried in the past, repressed memories that surface in collective dreams or nightmares. To plumb the depths of this historical psyche is the task that Abdoh sets for himself in work after work. Operationally, his process is not unlike that of an archeologist or a paleontologist, sifting through layers of accumulated thought and debris to get at something more structural, the root cause, if you will, of our current predicaments. At the same time, he is also the psycho-analyst of history, rewriting myths of the past, debunking contemporary myths and ready-made ideas, and in the process both adumbrating a collective unconscious and creating new myths or models for the future.

Unearthing these remains, whose laws are etched immutably in fragments from the past, demands painstaking research into history, both of the world and of the place the person occupies in that world. It is to Abdoh's credit that he gives us both with a vision and a scope unrivaled in the contemporary theater, excepting the works of director Robert Wilson and playwrights such as Heiner Müller and Charles L. Mee Jr., artists who mine the past for historical and mythic sources with which to illuminate the contemporary human condition. In his most recent work, *Quotations from a Ruined City,* a Hobbesian nightmare, the Los Angeles riots are framed within stories of the Pilgrims' settling into their new land, of greed and abundantly vulgar consumerism, of discipline (boot camp, Boy Scout, and concentration camp variety), urban decay and crime, and death. In *The Law of Remains,* Jeffrey Dahmer and Andy Warhol and journeys of the dead and the dying are initiated by a lynching staged under the plaintive sounds of a New England folk song, followed by urgent scenes of autos-da-fé, book burnings, black magic, and culminating in a football field set in heaven (or hell) with steel-framed hospital beds substituting for bleachers; in *Tight Right White,* the subject of race relations is explored within a frame (one of many) of black-exploitation films, minstrelsy, and plantation house lifestyles. Like his peers, Abdoh rummages through the detritus of the past, but unlike those who view it as a treasure trove of playthings to be recalled as fancy or fashion dictates, as neutral artifacts devoid of significance, Abdoh resurrects it painfully to remind us of who we once were and who we could all once again become.

The past, the dead, the remains must be retrieved and re-looked at if we are ever to gain insights into the present. Laws governing the present lie hidden in the secrets or the stilled voices and the remains of the buried. Death rules in the Abdoh universe, its reigning spirit that of Thanatos. In his theater we witness once again the birth of tragedy, the ritual model of theater answering the call of voices from the beyond. He dreams Artaud's plague into existence, that feverish intensity of being where mind and body, life and death merge in the service of art and of truth. If Virgil and Dante are his guides in this epic quest (structurally, Abdoh's plays often replicate the schematic patterns of *The Divine Comedy*), the path itself is that laid out in the Egyptian *Book of the Dead*. It is a search to make the fragments whole, not to let bygones be bygones, to attempt to answer questions left unanswered. In this sense, there is in Abdoh's artistry a deep-seated spiritual dimension, a desperate need for resurrection, to act against the inertia, the passivity, the dying that he witnesses all around him.

Abdoh's is indeed a theater of rage, a desire to seek out and manifestly display the raw nerves—psychic and cultural—that pulse beneath the seemingly tranquil surface of our culture. The anger, fueled by Nietzschean longings, vents its fury in Dionysian impulses, where Thanatos and Eros embrace in ecstatic couplings and the body becomes the preeminent sign of life and death. That this is undeniably so in the age of AIDS lends added poignancy to Abdoh's theatrical universe. But there is a larger frame at work here. Philosophically, the mind-body dualism, a legacy of the Enlightenment, is firmly situated at the center of Abdoh's concerns. He questions that dualism by juxtaposing it to non-Western philosophical and religious premises, the latter couched subtly in the varied physicality and gesturality of his actors' modes of presentation on stage. As with Artaud before him, Abdoh sees the place and function of the body in other cultures (including subcultures) as offering not only other models of being in the world, but as forced to embody in these bodies, these private selves, those values—spiritual and cultural—subjugated by the powers of society and the state. In the manner of ancient mystics and latter-day philosophers and artists (St. Augustine, Rousseau, Sade, Rimbaud, Artaud, Bataille, and Pasolini come to mind), Abdoh compels us to confront the body as the final repository of the play of forces that define the scope, purpose, and well-being of society and of a culture.

It is rare indeed to find an artist these days so passionately and unequivocally committed to both topical issues and a larger philosophical worldview. It is rarer still to find an artist in whom the belief that art, advanced art, by its very nature ought to be adversarial in spirit is so firmly entrenched. And just as gratifying is the realization that here is an artist who has chosen to build his theatrical foundations and his enormous craft on a sound knowledge of the history of his form, not only paying debts to the art practice of diverse cultures, but also carrying forward the tradition of the American avant-garde, namely Living Theatre, Richard Foreman, and the Wooster Group. His is an ecstatic art where passion and fury burn with grieved sorrow, where fervent love for his fellow beings struggles heroically against the destructive agencies of power and abuse. Reza Abdoh's is a voice that we dare not still, for he has had the courage, the supreme courage, to peer deep down into the abyss that surrounds us on all sides in these most treacherous of times.

Marvin Carlson

Back to the Basics

A quarter of a century has now passed since the revolutionary year of 1968. [. . .] From time to time [I] wonder if the more memorable experimental theater of that era was really so much more intense and provocative than more recent work, or whether the combination of my own youth at the time and nostalgia today has exaggerated its effect in the memory. Were the early Living Theatre productions really that gripping, the works of John Vaccaro and the early Charles Ludlam really that outrageous, *Dionysus in 69* really that provocative, Grotowski's *The Constant Prince* really that viscerally disturbing? Recent years have not been devoid of striking, even memorable experimental theater works in New York, but much of it seems, in comparison with my memories of the work of that earlier period, more intellectually abstract, more technological (if not technocratic). Even Richard Schechner's recent *Faust Gastronome,* which recalled the work of the late sixties in many ways, both positive (in its striking physical images) and negative (in its casual sexism), never, for me at least, generated the kind of physical excitement that I recall from the best work of the Performance Group at that time.

Just when I was about to conclude that either advancing age or postmodern abstraction had put me beyond the reach of that kind of visceral theater, along came the works of Reza Abdoh, to provide a salutary shock treatment for the New York experimental scene, and a welcome reminder of how stunning, dangerous, and provocative such theater can be. Abdoh's family emigrated from Iran to London, where he directed a National Youth Theatre production of *Peer Gynt* at the

Originally published in *Journal of Dramatic Theory and Criticism* 8, no. 2 (1993): 187–91.

age of 14, then to California, where his production of a radical restaging of *King Lear* in a small Los Angeles coffeehouse gained him the attention and support of the Los Angeles Theatre Center (LATC).

The first two parts of Abdoh's *Bogeyman Trilogy—The Hip-Hop Waltz of Eurydice* and *Bogeyman*—outraged, scandalized, and fascinated the audiences of the LATC and established Abdoh as one of America's most imaginative and provocative young directors. When the LATC closed, Abdoh moved his base of operations to New York, establishing here his own company, Dar A Luz. The third play in the *Bogeyman Trilogy, The Law of Remains,* was thus premiered in New York last season. Although New York has not yet, unhappily, hosted the rest of the trilogy, it had seen one previous example of the work of this gifted director, *Father Was a Peculiar Man,* an ambitious piece of site-specific theater presented in several blocks of the Manhattan meatpacking district in July of 1990 (reviewed in *JDTC,* Spring 1991).

Father Was a Peculiar Man, presented in an unknown part of the city in the middle of summer at a time when Abdoh's name was almost unknown here, did not attract a great deal of attention; but word of it, and of the *Bogeyman* plays in California, spread through the theater community. When *The Law of Remains* opened in midtown (in the semiderelict Diplomat Hotel) and in midseason, it became the most talked about experimental theater event of the year. *Tight Right White* has built upon that enthusiasm, and with Dar A Luz scheduled for a series of European performances, it seems very likely that Abdoh will soon become a significant figure in the international theatrical avant-garde.

Scarcely a review of Abdoh's two more recent New York works has failed to evoke Artaud (Michael Feingold's review of *Tight Right White* in the *Village Voice* bore the headline "Artaud You So"), and the overwhelming sensual assault of these productions, their thrusting upon the stage precisely those elements in our private imaginations and social constructions that we would most like to suppress (not to mention the frequent specific images of torture, graphic violence, and bloodshed) perhaps inevitably stimulate associations with Artaud's Theatre of Cruelty. In this respect, stunning and imaginative as it was both visually and spatially, *Father Was a Peculiar Man* was not quite representative of the main line of Abdoh's work. Despite visual references to the banal typical American family of the advertising world, or to the eruption of violence represented by the Kennedy assassination (literally reenacted in the district streets), the structuring of this work around Dostoyevsky's *Brothers Karamazov* necessarily pulled it away from the exploration of the American social psyche that informs the other works; and the sprawling, largely exterior performing space prevented the kind of concentration, even entrapment, of the audience that has contributed importantly to the power of the later, more enclosed works. Only in the last "station" of *Father*, when the audience was taken inside one of the packing and processing plants and left wandering in small, death-haunted rooms amid tableaux of nude and tortured bodies, did they enter the world that would make up the round of Abdoh's subsequent work.

As an HIV-positive gay artist who creates highly charged sexual and social material, Abdoh has inevitably been compared with such controversial artists as David Wojnarowicz, Tim Miller, Karen Finley, and Guillermo Gómez-Peña, and there are certainly points of similarity in the high level of intensity and the brutal foregrounding of the darkest secrets of our social organization. Yet despite some thematic overlap (for example, Reagan and AIDS are linked in the works of several of these artists, and mutilation and rape provide frequent images), Abdoh's creations develop their effects in quite a different way. Most obviously, they are always company works. Performance artists like Miller, Finley, and Gómez-Peña have from time to time worked with groups, but their most striking and memorable creations have almost always been solo pieces. Abdoh takes full advantage of a company approach, bombarding his audience with multiple stimuli often provided by actors working on several sides of the audience at once, supplemented by film and video projections. Related to this multiple focus is the relatively minor role played by directly autobiographical (or presumably autobiographical) material in Abdoh's creations. Abdoh, very widely read and highly thoughtful about his art, is well aware of the power of liberation and resistance culture and identity politics, and as an Oriental and gay, well positioned to utilize these. Nevertheless, even though the *Bogeyman* trilogy, with its no-holds-barred evocation of the dreams and nightmares of homosexuality in America, from tattooed naked chorus boys in a kick line to the grisly activities of Milwaukee serial killer Jeffrey Dahmer, inevitably suggests a relationship with Abdoh's sexual and sociocultural positioning, it does not really use this as a grounding in the way that Finley and others have done.

Tight Right White, though deeply implicated in American sexual and racial politics and phantoms, is even less an "autobiographical" meditation, but for that very reason allows a clearer glimpse of just how an

Abdoh piece operates. Each of the three New York productions has been based upon an organizing narrative: the Dostoyevsky novel for *Father,* an imaginary film of Jeffrey Dahmer's life by Andy Warhol for *The Law of Remains,* the 1975 blaxploitation film *Mandingo* for *Tight Right White.* Onto these structural frames Abdoh weaves a dazzling postmodern mélange of cultural references. Among the material utilized in *The Law of Remains* were the Egyptian *Book of the Dead,* American folk songs, Hitchcock films, World War II military songs, and baby-care videos, while *Tight Right White* utilizes slave narratives, minstrel routines, white supremacist documents (astonishingly, Abdoh managed to live for a while with a group of white supremacists in Idaho to gather material), German tales and folk songs, Punch and Judy shows, and a stand-up Borscht Belt comedian in a plaid fat suit and with a huge fake Jewish nose as a running narrator. His opening lines provide a touch of the show's free-wheeling satirical attack. "I think there was a day—first grade or second grade," he begins sentimentally, "when my best friend Carl hit me on the way home from school and said he wouldn't play with me anymore because I had killed Jesus." Taking his microphone over to a sweet little old lady in a shawl sitting in a rocking chair he continues that he told his mother of the incident. She rocks quietly for a moment, then mutters "Fuck the *shvartzers.* Fuck the *goyem.*"

In both productions, Abdoh's astonishing mix of material and of tone is evoked in stunning, overwhelming profusion, with monologues and dialogues often overlapping and so rapidly delivered as to challenge comprehension, the whole interspersed with a staggering variety of dance routines, circle and square dances, folk dances of all types, chorus kick lines (Abdoh loves these), ballroom dances, African dances, and so on, all executed at the same supercharged energy of the entire piece. The constant mixture of text, music, movement, video, film, and visual spectacle is disturbing, moving so rapidly as to defy analysis, even comprehension, and yet Abdoh's productions inevitably give a total impression not only of an astonishingly rich theatrical imagination but of an equally astonishing control of this complex material. Partly this is due to the way that the diverse material all relates back to key images and concerns, different in each work, and partly it is due to the use of repetition and variation of specific lines and images, building great poetic resonance in the course of the production. Two examples among many in *Tight Right White* are two interchanges from an ongoing TV interview between a black and the Jewish MC: "What's your name?"

"Blaster." "What's your tale?" "Nothing has changed." and "Pack your bags. You're going home." "This IS home."—simple phrases that gradually take on profound resonances.

Abdoh's multifocus productions would be impossible in a conventional theatrical space, and fortunately his producer, Diane White, has a remarkable gift for discovering virtually unknown flexible spaces in the heart of New York's various theater districts. The Hotel Diplomat, two floors of which were used for *The Law of Remains,* is on 46th Street, just a block from Times Square. Its stunning, now partially derelict top floor two-story ballroom, which Abdoh used for the "heaven" to which Dahmer (and the audience) ascended for the final scene, may be recalled by moviegoers as the ballroom in the early scenes of *Malcolm X,* though to the best of my knowledge it has not before been used as a theater venue. *Tight Right White* is staged on most of the sixth floor of a building on Lafayette Street in Greenwich Village, directly opposite the Public Theatre.

The audience moves to three different locations during the evening in this latter space, with action often almost totally surrounding them. In the first location, large open stages backed by multiple film projections are to the audience's right and left, with, in front, a sort of burlesque runway connecting these and two continually running TV monitors. Beyond the stage to the left is another lower performance area used mostly for supplementary dances, pantomimes, and lighting effects. Behind the audience (they must turn to see it) is a kind of puppet stage, two elongated slots in large flats, primarily used for the display of real and false heads that carry on conversations. In the second location, the audience moves so that the stage formerly on their left is now on their right, a small percussion band is behind them and a new stage, backed by complex revolving panels depicting Southern mansions on one side and the beating of slaves on the other. The original seating area can still be seen and serves now as another acting space. For the final scene, the audience moves to another corner of the building, where the action is essentially concentrated on a single large stage in front of them, but one divided into two levels and several acting areas. The effect throughout is one of multiple activity, but as I have noted before, the repetition of themes and images, the relationship of all elements to the central concern of racial tensions, and the often ironic effects of playing one element against another both spatially and temporally do not result in an ultimate feeling of frustration or confusion. Rather each spectator is provided with the means to put together a unique experience out of this rich mixture and to go away with the impression that, while much has inevitably been missed, so densely packed and so ingeniously conceived has the total spectacle been, a stunning whole continues to vibrate in the memory long afterward.

Philippa Wehle

Excerpts from *"Tight Right White:*

A Poetic Work of Mourning"

[. . .] *Tight Right White* takes the form of what Abdoh calls "a cross between a Minstrel Show and a Borscht Belt night club act." The action moves at a furious pace among five main playing areas. Two wooden platforms, connected by a ramp, are raised structures. Two other stages, the Plantation and the House of Forgotten Knowledge sets, are at floor level. A raked area enclosed by sliding panels provides the fifth set. To these, Abdoh adds still further playing possibilities. Moods shift on the Plantation set, for example, thanks to a backdrop of swinging panels painted with happy plantation scenes on one side, and a slave hanging from a tree on the other. A second floor above the House of Forgotten Knowledge stage provides space for another layer of multiple actions including the unfurling of an enormous American flag. Still another space is provided by two sliding panels containing cut-out openings in which a lively puppet show is performed with "talking heads." These panels slide open to reveal a Hollywood jungle set complete with natives dancing around the cauldron in which the slave Mead in *Mandingo* is to be boiled alive.

When the show begins, the audience is ushered into the former gymnasium and asked to sit on the floor between the two wooden platforms, in front of the connecting ramp. (Later, they will be asked to move quickly to the other playing areas.) To the left, a large black "woman" (played by Dana Moppins, a large black man wearing a plain beige-colored dress, black curly wig, and black galoshes) rocks on a chair, fanning herself nonchalantly, a galvanized pail at her side. She is Big Pearl, the slave girl "pleasured" by Hammond Maxwell in the *Mandingo* story. To the right, on the other side of the ramp, Moishe

Originally published in *TheatreForum,* no. 4 (Winter/Spring 1994): 57–59.

Pipik, played by Tony Torn, wearing a garish plaid suit, gold shoes, a fake nose, and a bright yellow curly wig, stands looking down at the floor, hands clasped. In front of him is a larger gold pail. Biting coins to test their authenticity, he pretends to throw them across the spectators' heads. As if by magic, a clink is heard from Big Pearl's pail. Pipik urinates into his pail and out pops a money tree. Someone is whistling "When the Moon Comes over the Mountain." To the far right of the spectators, a group of Ku Klux Klan members dance around a poor emaciated black fellow, dressed in shabby overalls with no shirt underneath. He jumps on Pipik's stage, performs cunnilingus on one of the KKK members while the others race behind the audience carrying Confederate flags.

The show—a wild ninety-minute romp punctuated by neo-Nazi, Holocaust, and Ku Klux Klan imagery, German folk dances, a Jewish wedding dance, cakewalks, and hip-hop—has begun.

Spectators are surrounded by constantly shifting images, created by a cast of quick-change artists playing multiple roles, and disoriented by Abdoh's merciless assault on the senses. They are clearly not expected to take it all in at once. It is not easy to keep up with the fevered pace of *Tight Right White* or with the multilayered action; indeed at times it seems impossible. Not only is the text delivered at break-neck speed in German, English, Spanish, and the heavy dialect of the *Mandingo* sections, but the music (much of it performed live at high decibels by Carlos Rodriguez) purposefully drowns out much of the dense dialogue. One minute the cast performs an unrestrained, funky, down-and-dirty dance on one side of the stage; the next they become a Jewish wedding party, performing a captivating celebratory dance on the Family Home set, where all seems well except for those window shades that suddenly snap up to reveal startling images of Ku Klux Klan rites. Within a matter of seconds, an Austrian dance, complete with slapping of thighs and happy faces, momentarily attracts our curiosity, but attention quickly shifts to a solo number by Tom Fitzpatrick playing a "Mammy" with red floral print skirt and red bandanna, wailing "Why did a stray bullet hit my boy's head?" Throughout, video monitors project images of fire and conflagration, dead bodies and buildings toppling, American flags and Al Jolsen, followed by nude dancers dancing together in a nudist camp. Brenden Doyle, naked, turns slowly on what appears to be a wheel of torture. Meanwhile, the *Mandingo* scenario unfolds at its own pace.

The ongoing mayhem is regularly punctuated with "Heil Hitler" salutes and cries of "Wake up dead man!" (the title of a collection of chain gang songs that inspired Abdoh) and "Who will be the witness?" Sexual postures and encounters of every stripe, from the obscene to the playful, offend, disturb, and amuse. An actor painted red, bends over, derrière to the audience, and shaves his balls; Blaster sodomizes Moishe Pipik. During the puppet show, a big black penis suddenly pops out through a hole in the panel at eye level with the audience; immediately a hand pops through another hole next to it and fondles it playfully. Other lighter moments of comic relief include the repeated appearance of Dana (in plaid skirt, pullover V-neck sweater, and blond page-boy wig) singing "I Have Confidence," from *The Sound of Music.*

There are forcefully moving, quiet moments as well—not too many, but enough to provide the necessary respites. There is James Williams's mournful singing of a Negro spiritual "I'm Going Home," and a love song sung by Holocaust prisoners in Auschwitz, plaintively rendered by Felix Fibich standing at the end of a corridor far to the left of the spectators and dressed in long black priestly robes.

Despite the complexity of *Tight Right White,* it is possible to pick out two essential stories running intermittently throughout the piece. One concerns the spiritual journey of Blaster, the principal character, the "black" man in overalls taunted by the KKK in the opening scene. He is a teenage junkie–drug dealer, "posed on the edge of who he is," in the words of Tom Pearl, the white actor who plays the role. He is "like every rebel kid shoved aside by society because society feels he's too much of a burden to it," says Abdoh. His face and body are loosely smeared with black paint so that his white skin shows through. "Is he black, is he white?" He doesn't really know. Nor does the audience.

The other main story follows Moishe Pipik, a combination Borscht Belt comic and TV producer who seems to be on a similar quest for self-knowledge and understanding. Loud and flashy with his gold loafers and large padded behind, Moishe, too, longs to understand who he is, but he appears less able to focus on his goal. Perhaps he is too busy trying to find the right "story to option." He is carried away by his power to give Blaster what he thinks he wants, for only Pipik can "open the gates for him, give him power, junk, money, control," make Blaster a TV idol. Still, underneath this blatant stereotype of the Jewish promoter/operator, we sense that he too longs to "come to grips with something," as Abdoh says, he too longs to find himself. [. . .]

In *Tight Right White,* Abdoh constantly forces the audience to question the precarious nature of identity and the insidious perpetuation of stereotyping in our society by consistently casting against type, race, and gender. Nothing, no one, is ever what one expects. Jewish wedding music is heard and the bride appears. It's Dana (who is male and black), her Scarlet O'Hara–type white lace wedding dress unbuttoned in the back, too tight for Dana's large frame. James Williams, a tall thin black actor wearing a white powdered wig and bell-bottom trousers with lace on the bottom, dances a quadrille with white actor Tom Fitzpatrick in breeches and boots. Jacqueline Gregg, a black actress, her face painted white with pink cheeks, plays blond Miss Blanche in the *Mandingo* scenes, and so on. According to costume and makeup designer Alix Hester, there are 150 costumes in all, along with 52 hats and 16 wigs, and at least 35 masks not to mention the painted faces. Costumes range from 1850s plantation/slave trader outfits to 1960s bell-bottoms and platform shoes; neo-Nazi overcoats, lederhosen, funk, and grunge with frequent combinations of several styles. In *Tight Right White,* stereotypes are not just dethroned, they are dismantled.

Ultimately, Blaster breaks away from the pull of fame and fortune. "I don't need your cookie," he declares to those around him who try to convince him otherwise. He'll manage, somehow, to find his own safe place, without any hand-outs from those in power. Moishe Pipik too has finally come to an understanding. Tired, cold, lonely, and hungry, he tells Blaster that he's ready to call it quits. He takes off his fat suit, removes the fake nose and picks up a suitcase as if to embark on his own personal journey. Signing off one last time, he bids a final farewell: "Here's to you, Blaster," he says, as if drinking a toast to Blaster's declaration of independence. "Good night, sweet Prince," he continues, "Here's Moishe Pipik sayink goodnight Missus, vere ever you are."

The play's final scene—an epilogue, in fact—highlights Blaster on a chair, wearing an oxygen mask, frantically gasping for air, desperately trying to get somewhere where he can be his own person, somewhere he can breathe freely. It is snowing and his gasps are increasingly magnified throughout the theater as he struggles on. In the background are four figures in huge carnival masks. One of these figures, Mister Tight Right White himself (in a white mask with a curled lip snarling viciously) points a threatening finger at Blaster. He is accompanied by Mrs. Tight Right White (a smaller white mask) and two black stereotypes in pickaninny clothing. Holding hands, they seem chained to each other forever in the cold, wintry night, an indomitable force from which Blaster must escape.

Directly across from them on the opposite stage, one dimly perceives a group roasting marshmallows at a campsite fire. The wood is running out, the world is in decay and collapse, but a child wonders at the shooting stars overhead as once more we hear "When the Moon Comes over the Mountain." When asked what will happen "When the Moon Comes over the Mountain," Abdoh replied: "As a people we'll be more aware of our obligations to each other, our potential, and how cruel the human race can be and how it can destroy the universe. It's the function of the arts to remain vital and inform."

Is this ending Abdoh's coda of hope? If so, it is melancholic and wistful. Indeed, underneath the circus, behind the vaudeville of *Tight Right White,* one senses a current of unfocused sadness. For Abdoh, *Tight Right White* is more than anything else "a *Trauerarbeit,* a poetic work of mourning . . . of longing for some kind of response, some kind of legitimate solution." However elusive the solutions and the response may be, the power of Abdoh's final images certainly suggests that new beginnings, however ambiguous, are possible.

John Bell

Excerpts from

"AIDS and Avant-garde Classicism: Reza Abdoh's

Quotations from a Ruined City"

I carry the ruined city under my skin.

—*Quotations from a Ruined City*

I admire your optimism. My pessimism is only a form of optimism. I would like things to happen differently from the way they do and I find myself weeping over ruins. Then I think that the ruins have great and surprising beauty and stimulate men in some unexpected direction within art. Cities in solid gold must sleep beneath the sands.

—Jean Cocteau, "Letter to Americans"

Reza Abdoh's work appears on the grid of late-twentieth-century American theater as both consummation and regeneration of the avant-garde tradition that has characterized innovative Western theater since French symbolism's rejection of realism one hundred years ago. Abdoh's work, and in particular his 1994 production, *Quotations from a Ruined City*, fits into the continuum of American experimental theater that, since the end of World War II, has led from the opening wedge of new theater practices created by the Living Theatre, John Cage, and Merce Cunningham in the 1950s; through the Judson Church performances of Yvonne Rainer and others, 1960s happenings, and the politicized experimental theater of the Vietnam era; to the high postmodernism of Robert Wilson, Richard Foreman, and the Wooster Group. Abdoh's productions, working in the same vein of image-text-sound performance that, since the days of Lugné-Poe's Théâtre d'Art has stood as the constant antithesis to Western stage realism, have appeared in New York, Los Angeles, and in Europe as a culmination of modernist and

Originally published in *TDR* 39, no. 4 (T148) (Fall 1995): 21–47.

131

postmodernist theaters' fragmented, multimedia collage technique, but also, in decided contrast to the content of postmodern performance, as a significant step outside (or beyond) the disconnected neutrality post-modernist theater cultivated as its ideological means of survival.[1] [. . .]

Reza Abdoh's assaultive combination of nonstop live action, star-tlingly rich yet enigmatic text, very loud music, and surprising bursts of disconnected film and video images appeared to some audience mem-bers like the obscure rantings of an avant-garde muse gone over the edge into baroque indulgence. While Abdoh's penchant for "great vi-sual eloquence" was generally praised by admirers and detractors alike, critical opinion fell on either side of the question of what it all means: whether Abdoh was creating coherent theater, or, as Ondrej Hrab, the director of Prague's Archa Theater said to me upon seeing Abdoh's *Tight Right White* (1993), simply "vomiting ideas." Abdoh's presentation of image and sound certainly had the explosive, excretive quality of Hrab's metaphor. The question about whether Abdoh was a "theatrical genius or just another crank peddling a vision"[2] is answerable when one considers the meaning of the symbolic fragments forming what Robert Sember calls an "unstoppable river of information," Abdoh's "catastro-phe that takes an hour and a half."[3] Experiencing *Quotations from a Ru-ined City*, as Sember sees it, is like being caught in a controlled explo-sion of information made that much more powerful by its tight compression of symbols and its ability to work on several different lev-els simultaneously. The images in Abdoh's theatricality register in the psyche on a subliminal level to connect with each other and with the bank of images anyone exposed to United States–based mass culture carries with them, willingly or unwillingly. To a visitor from eastern Eu-rope not yet over-drenched in American culture, the spectacle might indeed appear as a disgorgement of ideas. But, as one could say of Czech surrealist filmmaker Jan Svankmajer's similar image explosions, the more one understands their source, the more the disparate images and the disparate ideas make sense.

Quotations from a Ruined City

Abdoh's *Quotations from a Ruined City* is a ninety-minute multimedia spectacle performed by twelve members of his Dar A Luz ensemble. Centering action on a raised downstage platform bordered by a low, white picket fence and separated from the audience by eleven horizontal strands of barbed wire, *Quotations* is a 1994 state-of-the-world address, a *theatrum mundi* incessantly presenting Abdoh's paradoxical point of view: the perpetual outsider who happened to be, as Abdoh described himself, "a TV junkie," immersed in and fixated on the multiple levels of signification in which American culture does its work.[4] Two male couples form the character focus of the show. Tom Fitzpatrick and Tony Tom, dressed first as Puritans and later as modern businessmen in corporate ties and blue blazers, are the capitalist entrepreneurs of a postapocalyptic world. Tom Pearl and Peter Jacobs, initially dressed all in white and then in green shirtwaist dresses, are the queer lovers locked in a sometimes abusive relationship. These two couples are in transit through the ruined city.

Sensory Overload

Quotations consists of sequences that alternate repetitive tableaux, group and solo scenes, and frenetic dance numbers choreographed in a frontal, MGM movie musical style by Ken Roht. Abdoh skillfully designed stage images from his rich visual vocabulary, which combined costume, objects, gesture, and a raw, physical acting style in an incessantly compelling high theatricality. Jarring juxtaposition—a classic avant-garde device more surrealist than postmodern—was Abdoh's usual method here.

In addition to the downstage platform and a floor-level upstage playing area, Abdoh completed the performance space with two video monitors and two rear-projection film screens, both hung above the stage. These sporadically burst into a profusion of found images with startling intensity, an intensity matched (or bettered) by a similarly jarring montage of sounds.

The controlled explosion of information comes at the audience on multiple levels. For example, near the end of the play the entire cast stands downstage right, dressed in Boy Scout uniforms (some with skirts instead of shorts), and sings a folk song, "When I First Came to This Land," with accompanying hand gestures. The video screens show a succession of farm animals (pig, goose, goat, etc.) sitting in a suburban living room. On the platform stage left, naked, the two lovers at the center of the show's focus (Tom Pearl and Peter Jacobs) "simulate," as a stage direction puts it, "tender fucking," quite realistically. The odd pastoral serenity of the uniformed Boy Scouts (men in skirts, women in shorts) singing an immigrants' song in the company of barnyard animals is in itself so striking that in several of the performances I witnessed, half the audience did not even notice the two lovers. The stage was so loaded with other images, and the audience so enervated by the experience of the preceding eighty minutes, that the startling scene of homosexual lovemaking simply existed on the periphery. This is probably how Abdoh wanted the image to work on stage: queer sexual congress presented not as a centered, sensational act, but as an everyday act of passion: decentered, simply occupying its own space, just part of the terrain. [. . .]

Horrors of War

The fifty-two scenes constituting *Quotations from a Ruined City* are mostly centered on American themes and American places, specifically Los Angeles and New York (although it is not correct to say that the play "takes place" in any specific locale), with periodic forays into Bosnia and Iraq. This geographic range is matched by the show's mythic time span, which begins with the patriarchal Tony and Tom F. in Puritan dress, and ends with them in modern blazers and ties. Civilization, or more accurately civilizations, are not happy bearers of progress here. The scene titles of *Quotations* give an idea of the pain and meanness each different locale, each different milieu, is capable of doling out to its inhabitants or its enemies: "Shackle Tableau," "Ear Pull Section," "Impalement," "Body Bag Sequence," "Dental Torture." [. . .]

One of the most uncomfortable sections of the production, and one which most specifically directs itself to contemporary political events, is the "Impalement" scene, a narrative early in the show that describes (but does not depict) the torture of Mustafa, a Bosnian Muslim, by Serbians. A herd of life-size cut-out sheep has been set up on the Palermo stage; overhead on the video monitors is a montage of amateur-looking video footage of Beirut and Sarajevo—the most extensive literal images of ruined cities in the show. Broken up into short lines, the gruesome description of Mustafa's torture is spoken in alternating phrases by Fitzpatrick, Torn, Pearl, Jacobs, and Sabrina Artel, as each actor in turn picks up one of the sheep to drop off the upstage side of the platform:

TOM P.: On the ground was an oak pole, two and a half meters long, with a sharp iron point.

TONY: When they ordered Mustafa to lie down he lowered his head, then the Chetniks walked up to him and started stripping off his coat and shirt.

SABRINA: Then they tied each of his legs with a rope.

TOM P.: Two Chetniks pulled his legs wide apart.

PETER: Another Chetnik rested the pole against two logs so the pole's top was between Mustafa's legs.

TONY: He pulled a short, wide dagger out of his belt, kneeled before the outstretched body of Mustafa and cut the cloth of his trousers between his legs to widen the opening where the pole would enter the body.[5]

And so on. The first scene interruption is "12 seconds of sound": excruciatingly loud industrial shrieks. The projected images shift from video to black and white film, including footage of a cymbal player. The scene resumes, is interrupted for sixteen more seconds of the same aural assault, and then concludes with a description of Mustafa, impaled on the pole six feet above the ground, growling "Chetniks I hope you die like dogs . . . die like dogs . . . die like dogs."

The vivid description of torture causes the audience immediate discomfort. This is due to a number of factors, perhaps most important the fact that, despite his uninhibited capability of presenting such images, Abdoh shows nothing of what is being described. Instead, the audience is forced to imagine. The visual field balances the actors' aggressive competition for the cut-out sheep with the video images of shelled-out modern buildings. These juxtaposed visual images of ordinary daily life (the pastoral sheep, the actors doing their work, the calm and distanced documentary effect of the home-video footage of blasted architecture) make the textual horror that much stronger.

Despite the constant presence of the Bosnian War in news media and hints of potentially increased U.S. and U.N. military involvement in it, the war hardly surfaced in New York avant-garde theater during the winter of 1994.[6] So Abdoh's powerful focus on it was unusual, a reminder that disastrous international political situations could be legitimate subject matter for theater. However, Abdoh, who might be expected to support the Muslim and multiethnic side of the conflict against the recrudescence of European racist ideology in the Serbian operations of "ethnic cleansing," did not approach the issue with the simplistic zeal (mistakenly) ascribed to agitprop theater. His response to the atrocities of the Bosnian War was distanced, nearly nonpartisan, almost elegiac. A few scenes before the "Impalement" section, Artel, clad in a Puritan matron's costume, wields an axe while reciting a definition of "Chetnik" (the Bosnian name for Serb militants, originally applied to fascist Serb paramilitary groups in the Second World War). Artel's definition is biting, but hyperbolically extreme:

> SABRINA: *(Enters with an axe.)* "Be civil, will you!" Chetnik: The word derives from the one used for troop. There are several features characteristic of Chetniks. They tell lies. They are Serbs. They massacre the Bosnians. Through slaughtering, killing, burning, raping, and robbing the Chetniks hope to conquer the country of Bosnia. The Chetniks are defenders of the Serbian cause. The Serbian cause is all things Serbian: men, women, birds, fish, plants, and the Serbian Crow. Serbian Crow. Serbian Crow.[7]

[. . .] While on the one hand Abdoh pushed his theatrical images into the controversial area of partisan politics (a move always suspect in American theater, except when the politics express accepted ideologies), he simultaneously stepped back to critique all politics: inhuman use of torture as well as the simplistic cant of the political ideologue seeking to define her/his opponent as evil. In this way, Abdoh retained some of high postmodernism's skepticism of politics in general, and yet dove into the messy area of post–Cold War geopolitics without hesitation.[8] [. . .]

Repetition and Intent

[. . .] Like seventies minimalism, avant-garde movements of the early twentieth century often allowed the form of their work to stand as message, an effective strategy at a moment when abstraction and collage—simply by themselves—could produce splendid outrage in audiences unaccustomed to considering such forms as "real" art. Abdoh's work, at the other end of the century, abides in a very different environment, addressing an audience almost exclusively immersed in montage, collage, and the intense symbolism of advertising, especially through television. Faced with a culture in which abstraction and collage are normative, Abdoh combined nonlinear structure with subversive subject matter in *Quotations* to address issues of patriarchy, religion, intolerance, will, and desire. In order to deliver various fragments of content through nonlinear structure, Abdoh used repetition and variation on many different levels.

Repeated dances, phrases, images, and sounds—especially when they call up unpleasant images of ugly, brutal humanity—are wearying. But they succeed in defining a landscape, in creating a theatrical world which, Abdoh has shown, mirrors the real world all too well. Abdoh's fugue structure balances repetition with variation skillfully enough to maintain audience interest. [. . .] And despite Abdoh's embrace of disorienting, seemingly chaotic structure, there is in fact a little story, a little progression, a little character development, a little plot—as there must be when the same characters appear on stage for ninety minutes.

By the end of *Quotations,* Torn and Fitzpatrick have transformed from Puritan dress to modern suits, and then (worn down by the abuses of the play to weary, disheveled businessmen) to rumpled shirtsleeves, ties askew, both wearily leaning on long staffs. They slap each other—for Abdoh, a typical act of abusive intimacy—but then drop their staffs and kiss.

They and the rest of the cast, except Pearl and Jacobs, crank up their "Final Dance," a last frenetic clog and tap number in which couples (one performer on each side of the stage) methodically remove the eleven strands of barbed wire separating them from the audience. This is a preparation for their last burst of activity, a leap offstage into the audience for a final exit through the house. Pearl and Jacobs slowly approach each other, fall to their knees, and embrace in a single spotlight, as their taped voices recite the last speech, a dream:

> TOM/PETER: I am in a beautiful garden. As I reach out to touch the flowers they wither under my hands. A nightmare feeling of desolation comes over me as a great dragon-shaped cloud darkens the earth. A few may get through the gate in time. Remember. Remember. We are bound to the past as we cling to the memory of the ruined city.[9]

At the end, *Quotations from a Ruined City* turns, as it has intermittently throughout the performance, to a tender personal moment, probably important for Abdoh as it was for Abdoh's characters. The smallest modicum of "story" here—the slight development of the Pearl/Jacobs relationship, the consistency of their love—is romantic and peaceful, a bittersweet coming together. It is not a "real" happy ending, but a passably happy one, not unlike what Hollywood might do if it made 1990s MGM-style musicals about queer young men finding strength and spiritual redemption. But Abdoh was not content to let romance reign alone. Following the men's embrace, the last illuminated image is four larger-than-life-size sides of beef hanging upstage: dead meat.

Hafiz and Symbolism, Ta'ziyeh and Death

[. . .] Hafiz is considered the premier lyric poet in the Persian language.[10] According to Abdoh, "there isn't a single Iranian that doesn't know Hafiz."[11] Abdoh used one of Hafiz's mystic poems about eternity in *Quotations,* its Farsi characters calligraphed in gold letters on large, black, stick-mounted cards topped by a reclining crescent. But it is clear that Persian poetry was not only a textual and thematic touchstone for Abdoh but a structural one as well. Hafiz's writing offers a clue into Abdoh's use of what he called "multilayered reality."

Influenced by Sufi mysticism, Hafiz's pantheistic poetry employs an elaborate, conventionalized symbol system that in many ways conflicts with orthodox Islam because of the poems' hedonistic bent. All of Hafiz's couplet-based *ghazels* have at least three levels of signification, working simultaneously as celebrations of love and wine, as Sufi mystic theology, and as sexually symbolic odes to a divine male lover.[12] The poetry of Hafiz has enthused and confused Westerners (beginning with Goethe, who adapted some of it in *West-ostlicher Divan*), because the couplets from which Hafiz constructs his *ghazels* are thematically distinct but symbolically unified. Based on discontinuous, psychological associations rather than linear development, Hafiz's poetry has been compared to that of the French symbolist poets Mallarmé, Valéry, and Rimbaud. In 1968 a Western critic even proposed that Hafiz, in the fourteenth century, had in fact "introduced," *avant la lettre,* "'modernism' into Persian literature."[13]

The other major Iranian cultural influence on Abdoh's work was Ta'ziyeh, the Shi'i Muslim tradition of processions and martyr plays performed annually during the ten-day Muslim festival of Muharram.[14] Ta'ziyeh, Abdoh said, had "a great deal of influence" on his work, and the connections between the two are strong. Formally, Ta'ziyeh features a broad, stylized acting technique emphasizing histrionic gesture and declamatory speech. Each Ta'ziyeh play of the ten-day cycle is a mourning ritual centered on the liminal event of death—of Husayn (grandson of Mohammed and an Imam of Shi'i Islam), or of specific members of Husayn's family and entourage. Commemorations of death and occasions for symbolic community mourning, Ta'ziyeh plays have had no exact equivalent in Europe since fifteenth-century Christian martyr plays and cycle dramas were regularly performed (contemporary Central American passion plays, however, do offer an interesting comparison). [. . .]

As in Hafiz's poetry, part of what Abdoh calls Ta'ziyeh's "hyperreality" consists of its ability to exist simultaneously in three modes of time and space ("literal," "representational," and "non-time") which "totally interpenetrate each other."[15] Ta'ziyeh's depiction of "real" events in heightened circumstances so fraught with emotion that they provoke a true Greek tragedy catharsis was emulated by Abdoh, who wished to bring the same kind of experience to his audiences, although they may not "believe" in the ritual efficacy of theater the way Shi'i audiences in Iran believe in Ta'ziyeh. This made Abdoh's search for a collective sensitive nerve in his audience that much more intense, and when he found the nerve, he produced shocks. This is a way (or perhaps the only way) to engender a cathartic effect in an audience of nonbelievers. Today's theater audiences, in Abdoh's opinion, arrive "ready to detach" themselves from the performance experience. However,

> when the experience forces them, or invites them, to de-detach themselves from what they are witnessing, then I think the relationship of the viewer to the event is a genuine relationship. And they can interpret it, they can read it in certain different ways. They can emotionally respond to it. They can become a part of it. They can hate it. They can think it's crap, whatever. But it's impossible for them to be in a state of stasis. So it's movement that I'm after. An infusion of a radical or a subtle shift in their perception.[16]

Abdoh's desire here—to persuade an audience to participate in a transformative ritual process—parallels the function of Ta'ziyeh for Muslim audiences in Iran.

Abdoh saw in Ta'ziyeh "a certain kind of struggle to reach divinity," to reach "purification and redemption, through the act of sacrifice and through the act of performance."[17] The act of sacrifice Ta'ziyeh focuses on, of course, is death, and the way death is treated in Ta'ziyeh has important ramifications for the contemporary theater of death which AIDS has engendered, and of which Abdoh's post-HIV+ plays are an important part. In Ta'ziyeh, death is an inevitable end and the details of its process are the center of dramatic focus—even more so than in Greek tragedy. Death is the central action of Ta'ziyeh, and its complications, its details, its outrages, and its ability to arouse deep emotions of love are all important elements in the theater of death Abdoh has created. Mass-media performances of death in the West tend to trivialize, in most cases, its metaphysical importance. But Ta'ziyeh, somewhat parallel to nineteenth-century neogothic sensibilities (and certainly those of Edgar Allen Poe, one of Abdoh's favored writers and an important theorist for French symbolists), focuses on the act of death, pauses over its minutiae, ponders its meaning, and, as Abdoh has said, finds redemption and significance in it.

Quotations from a Ruined City, also focusing on the nature of decay and death, was an intensely personal response by Abdoh to his own approaching end. The deaths in Ta'ziyeh are martyrs' deaths; this is also an important link to Abdoh's theater. Martyrdom raises the importance of death to a higher level; unjust, yet not unexpected, the martyr's death immediately assumes significance in a greater context, becomes meaningful on a different, higher plane. Abdoh transferred Ta'ziyeh's method of making great sense of death from an environment (Iran) and religion (Islam) no longer hospitable to him, to a new context in a society struggling over the meaning of AIDS.

AIDS and Postmodernism

Abdoh's theater work, especially his post-HIV+ productions with his Dar A Luz company, marks a significant break with high-postmodernist theater as represented by Wilson, Foreman, and the 1980s work of the Wooster Group. Postmodern cultural theory of the 1980s proposed or rationalized a retreat from point-of-view as a logical response to the collapse of aesthetics into politics. At that time, Hal Foster, for example, argued that engaged political art, "locked in a rhetorical code," was "problematic" in late-twentieth-century Western society, where "there can be no simple representation of reality."[18] Foster's reading of the representational incertitude of late-twentieth-century society mirrors Roland Barthes's description, in a discussion of literary theory, of the "truly revolutionary" act of "refusing to fix meaning."[19] Philip Auslander expanded Foster's defense of incertitude in an analysis of the Wooster Group's postmodernist landmark, *Route 1 & 9,* which, Auslander said, was in part a response to the "crisis" of political theater precipitated by "the obvious inappropriateness of the political art strategies left over from the historical avant-garde of the early twentieth century and from the 1960s."[20] In postmodernist theater the refusal to fix meaning is concurrent with a steadfast attention to form over content, or, when the question of content becomes inevitable, with the embrace of irony as the only viable point of view. [. . .]

Postmodernist theater's disengagement from the conviction that theater had the capacity to offer active, critical analyses of society (a conviction that, on and off, has characterized avant-garde theater since its inception in the 1890s) happened to coincide with, or perhaps inspired, increased support for avant-garde theater by large corporations nationwide, including AT&T and the Philip Morris Companies, the latter of which launched the Brooklyn Academy of Music's Next Wave Festival in 1984. This cultural effort joining corporate funders and arts organizations endured the disgrace of failing to raise $2.6 million for the complete production of Wilson's *the CIVIL warS* at the 1984 Olympic Arts Festival in Los Angeles, but still continues gamely into the end of the century in its effort to define avant-garde theater as a body of eternally new, international "landmark" productions.

Enter AIDS. The AIDS epidemic changed the nature of avant-garde performance irrevocably, forcing artists to consider and analyze not only the horror of the killing disease, but the social and political implications of government and corporate responses to the epidemic, as well as the questions of homophobia and racism inevitably linked with the AIDS crisis. The unavoidable presence of death through AIDS engendered artistic response, just as the Vietnam War in the 1960s, the rise of fascism in the 1930s, and the horrors of World War I in the teens had engendered avant-garde political theater throughout this century. Beginning with the brilliant political performance actions of ACT-UP, and the AIDS-conscious works of such gay men as Larry Kramer, Marlon Riggs, Robert Mapplethorpe, and David Wojnarowicz, a whole body of late-twentieth-century avant-garde performance came into definition, a body of work which, once again, demanded that common individual concerns connect to larger social and political issues. This change of focus is probably the single most important factor in the development of what might inelegantly be termed post-postmodernist performance.

The signs of this change are evident in the work of Ron Vawter (d. 1993), one of the American avant-garde's most brilliant performers. One of Vawter's last works, his solo performance *Roy Cohn / Jack Smith*, differed greatly from such Wooster Group productions as *Route 1 & 9* (which attempted the impossible task of deliberating the question of race in the United States without defining a point of view) and *North Atlantic* (which made an ill-fated attempt to consider the Dutch antinuclear movement while maintaining postmodernist disinterest). *Roy Cohn / Jack Smith*'s depiction of two very different HIV+ gay men— one (Cohn) steadfastly denying his sexuality, the other (Smith) openly using it to help in the joyous creation of Queer Theater—used the whole range of postmodern performance techniques refined by the Wooster Group, wedded them to a surprisingly realistic (almost naturalistic) aesthetic, and produced a theater production brilliantly combining both personal interests and political concerns.[21] Reza Abdoh similarly established the presence of AIDS within a larger grid of social, cultural, and political power relations, but Abdoh had more time on stage than Vawter or Smith to focus and develop his analysis of the meaning of AIDS.

Abdoh's work came at a particularly important time in twentieth-century theater, a moment when the ongoing traditions of Western avant-garde performance created over the past hundred years once more realigned themselves to adjust to changing circumstances: the end of the Cold War and its attendant crises of ideology; the struggle with AIDS; the adjustment of leftist 1960s social goals of equality to a situation of prolonged, indefinite, and uncertain struggle against institutional inertia and strong conservative reaction.

"Structural Stability" of the Avant-Garde

To the alarm of some of his critics, Abdoh's work actively and consciously recycled twentieth-century avant-garde performance techniques just as, in true postmodern fashion, it actively and consciously deconstructed and recycled images and sounds from the juggernaut of United States mass-media culture. In *Quotations from a Ruined City,* the barbed wire separating the audience from the stage echoes the Living Theatre's similar use of chain-link fence in its 1963 production *The Brig.*[22] Abdoh's use of strong, white, audience-focused stage lighting and obliquely significant scenic elements refers to the work of Richard Foreman. *Quotations'* sudden manic dance sequences and persistent video images follow Wooster Group techniques. There is something of both Robert Wilson and Peter Brook (two early influences) in the flow and scale of Abdoh's work, and his lugubrious, cryptic dialogue scenes, in turn, suggest both Beckett and Genet. Abdoh himself acknowledged particular debts to Duchamp and Breton, as well as to Symbolist poetry.

The problem with Abdoh's work, according to some critics, is that he recycled avant-garde techniques into pastiche constructions only capable of quoting the far greater works of recent postmodernist theater. This point of view parallels the critique of avant-garde art as an attack on the institution of bourgeois art,[23] an attack that—despite all its intentions—inevitably reinforces that very institution. According to Peter Bürger, for example, avant-garde art never developed its own style precisely because the whole purpose of avant-garde was (and is) to *negate* style.[24] Bürger sees avant-garde productions as one-time-only gestures, "acts of provocation" which, once completed, defy repetition or variation.[25] Once Duchamp made a urinal a "work of art," there is no reason to repeat the gesture, nor, furthermore, is the gesture even artistically possible. From the viewpoint of this critical position, avant-garde production *by definition* has no chance of developing continuity (i.e., a continuing theatrical language) and its successful works cannot or should not help engender others.

The "one-time-gesture" theory of avant-garde art precludes an understanding of avant-garde technique as a repository of tradition and continuity. The approach does, in some ways, clarify the historical avant-garde's sometimes oppositional relationship to normative culture and power, but only partially, since it fails to take into account the important ways avant-garde techniques have infused themselves into normative culture, for example into fascist and other forms of state-approved art, or into mass-media aesthetics, where a urinal (or at least a toilet) *will* appear again as a work of art, as the animated centerpiece of a bathroom disinfectant advertisement whose aesthetics are based on classic avant-garde techniques: collage, montage, and radical juxtaposition. Second, the one-time-gesture theory denies the possibility of a developing avant-garde aesthetic—which is what Reza Abdoh's work represents.

Abdoh's construction out of fragments is not only typical of postmodernist structure and of the modernist avant-garde in general, but characteristic of even older (and similarly misunderstood) traditions of European art going back to the baroque, as Walter Benjamin pointed out in *The Origin of Tragic Drama:*

> That which lies here in ruins, the highly significant fragment, the remnant, is, in fact, the finest material in baroque creation. For it is common practice in the literature of the baroque to pile up fragments ceaselessly, without any strict idea of a goal, and, in the unremitting expectation of a miracle, to take the repetition of stereotypes for a process of intensification. The baroque writers must have regarded the work of art as just such a miracle. And if, on the other hand, it seemed to be the calculable result of the process of accumulation, it is no more difficult to reconcile these two things than it was for the alchemist to reconcile the longed-for miraculous "work" and the subtle theoretical recipes. The experimentation of the baroque writers resembles the practice of the adepts. The legacy of antiquity constitutes, item for item, the elements from which the new whole is mixed. Or rather: is constructed. For the perfect vision of this new phenomenon was the ruin.[26]

Abdoh's productions are similarly "baroque" in the affirmative sense of the term Benjamin sought to establish in his recuperative study of seventeenth-century German drama, similarly concerned with contemplating the meaning of ruins and asserting that meaning through emblems and symbols rather than through realism. Different, perhaps, than the theater Benjamin was analyzing, Abdoh's productions tethered their multileveled symbolism to their director's harsh intent to "say something" through performance; this purpose puts his theater in sync with the politicized avant-garde theaters of the twentieth century.

Avant-garde performance, beginning with symbolism in the late nineteenth century, placed itself outside the existing structures of modern theater because of its desire to oppose rationalism and realism. Avant-garde theater artists discovered existing traditions of nonrational, nonrealistic performance in "low-culture" Western theater and in Asian and African theater, and stole or recycled elements of those performance traditions to create their own Symbolist, Futurist, Dadaist, Constructivist, Ballets Russes, Bauhaus, *Ausdrucktanz,* and modern dance productions. This technique allowed avant-garde artists the dangerous possibility of shopping in the supermarket of international culture but denied them the privilege of working from a solid performance *langue* in order to create their individual *paroles* (a privilege which non-Western performance practices did share with nominative Western performance traditions such as realistic drama). Frantisek Déak, writing about Prague School approaches to theater, clarifies this problem of avant-garde performance practice:

> In avant-garde theater, the breaking of particular conventions is often present, but the investigation of the avant-garde theater's own assumptions, conventions or "language" does not occur because the opposite of "language," the individual innovative act ("speech" in Saussurian terms), is of primary importance. Only in the strongly codified theater forms of the oriental and folk theater is the distinction of language and speech clearly visible.[27]

At the close of the twentieth century, however, avant-garde performance has indeed established a language, an aesthetic tradition built from a hundred years of piecing together performance fragments and shards of performing techniques into what Abdoh called "a kind of a vocabulary that everybody sort of shares."[28] In "Dynamics of the Sign in the Theater" Jindrich Honzl refers to the "structural stability" of "theaters with a centuries-old tradition"; a "constancy of structure" which "causes theatrical signs to develop complex meanings."[29] While a solidified structure might be thought to inhibit innovation, in Honzl's opinion "the immutability of the structure's key points does not necessarily impoverish its expressivity because within this traditional structure subtler and finer changes can take place."[30] What we ought to consider now is the fact that "avant-garde" theater has now created its own century-old tradition. What some may see as "cliché turns of performance art" in productions "self-conscious of [their] avant-garde roots" might, in fact, constitute theater that realizes that "avant-garde" performance has achieved its own "structural stability," through which a different type of theatrical art may be created.

While high postmodernist performance attempted an avant-garde strategy of opposition by means of form alone, proposing that disjunction, abstraction, and nonlinearity by themselves (without the aid of content) create antitheses of nominative society, Abdoh's work embodies a very different avant-garde approach. Instead of seeing conventional cultural "language" as a unitary monolith best opposed by individual "speeches" of deconstructed theater productions, Abdoh's work has opposed conventional culture and the power structures it represents by presenting avant-garde style as its own "language," a tradition of performance as dependent upon its particular structure as Western opera, *wayang kulit*, or Yoruba ritual are dependent on their structures. Working confidently within the established theater language of the twentieth-century avant-garde, Abdoh freed himself to return to political, social, and spiritual content in a way normally unavailable to high-postmodernist performance. In this sense, Abdoh's work has confounded the view of avant-garde performance as gesture. Instead, like the productions of any artist working within an established (but mutable) frame, Abdoh's theater demands to be considered as a particular combination of and variation on existing formulas. With Abdoh's Dar A Luz productions, avant-garde performance becomes "classic," and the creative possibilities of the avant-garde artist play in a very different space than they did at the previous turn of the century.

Quotations and "The Spectacle of AIDS"

Timothy Wiles writes that in 340 BCE the Greek actor Polos "made a great impact" in the role of Sophocles' *Electra* "when he carried the ashes of his own son into the theater in the urn supposed by Electra to carry the ashes of Orestes."[31] Performance in our time makes a similar impact, as HIV+ artists who decide to talk about AIDS put the questions of disease and death before their audiences. The subject of AIDS has naturally found a form in solo monologue, the signature technique of performance art in the 1980s. Abdoh himself made brilliant use of the form in "a very personal monologue"[32] performed by Mario Gardner in *Quotations from a Ruined City:*

MARIO: [. . .] And when the graves start yielding up the dead. I'll rise like Christ in drag and you best not offend me with your innocence, sister, because I bet you could tease a queen to death without half trying, so stop trying and let me tell you something. You reckon I ought to have a lot of regrets, my orgasm like being directly plugged in my hypothalamus socket and all, and my body in ruins after years of abuse but I have just one regret I never made a drop of whiskey in all my life and if I last long enough I'll remedy that. And the preacher came in right after my old buddy left. Asked me if I was ready to go. Ready to go? I put my mascara on, my lipstick on and my yellow pumps and I snapped back. I'll go when I'm good and ready. There were so many things I wanted to say to my old buddy. But this haze I'm in bedimmed from the ailment and all. I just sort of wander in and out of things. I did tell him I love him though. I remember telling him that. I never could have told him years back. Even though I should have. Funny how men have trouble telling each other things like that. Until the pale horseman starts to gallop by the door. Gallop. Gallop. Gallop. Gallop. Gallop.[33]

In Abdoh's work, the AIDS monologue does not stand alone but is instead a theatrically effective moment in a multidimensional spectacle. *Quotations from a Ruined City,* a theater production suffused at almost every instant with the sense of AIDS, is, surprisingly, not specifically about AIDS. Instead of following the performance artist's strategy of intense self-focus, Reza Abdoh decenters AIDS to focus instead on: the institutional abuses of familial and social patriarchy; the nature of queer identity and its role in and against normative society; the conflicts of New World Order capitalism as they materialize in America; the dangers of combining religious fundamentalism with politics and economics (fundamentalist Christianity, fundamentalist Islam); the persistent presence and importance of folk culture, especially in contrast to mass-media performance; and how the deconstruction of mass-media culture can help create a radical critique of that culture.

AIDS is not the central focus of *Quotations from a Ruined City,* but it infuses the work, operating (unnamed) as a central metaphor of ruin, the ruin of the body encompassing and standing for the ruins of modern society. Gordy and Floyd, the lovers and central characters of *Quotations,* are never defined as HIV+, but they seem to be, could be, probably are, especially in the context of the horrid hospital scene where medical treatment slips over into torture. Mario Gardner's monologue is the most explicit expression of an HIV+ point of view, but the expression is oblique. This is not at all the territory of Larry Kramer's outrage or ACT-UP's splendid and effective agitprop. Gordy and Floyd

seem to be in an endless flight from, or journey through, the intercon-
nected landscape of ruined cities, defined visually, textually, and aurally
on the Dar A Luz stage. Their bodies are signs of the HIV+ body, and
not so much symbols (signs with an arbitrary relationship to an abstract
signified) as they are indices (signs pointing to the physiological whole
that is their referent). They represent Abdoh's HIV+ body, the bodies of
other company members who may be HIV+, the bodies of gay men
and all those at risk, the bodies of everyone who faces death.

Like a poem by Hafiz, or a surrealist collage, Abdoh's theater not
only works simultaneously on different levels of reality, but believes in
those different levels. In this way, one of the most romantic scenes of
Quotations from a Ruined City is the "Medieval Hyperzone," where
Tom Pearl's character, apparently ill, and having removed a green dress
he has been wearing, slowly and painfully stumbles naked from stage
left to stage right, where Peter Jacobs stands, wearing only a medieval
helmet and holding an upraised sword. An aria from Wagner's
Tannhäuser plays, the two film screens above are filled with factory images, and Jacobs' sword implies some violent conclusion, but the scene
completes itself with a dramatic release when Jacobs drops the sword
and Pearl falls into his arms. The abusive violence that seems always to
characterize Abdoh's depiction of love dissolves in an embrace. In the
"Medieval Hyperzone" love is possible, and this possibility on a distant
level of existence implies hope for the same on our immediate level of
existence.

Dar A Luz actor Tom Fitzpatrick commented on the shows Abdoh
created after he tested positive for HIV in 1989, calling them his "angry
shows."[34] [. . .] But *Quotations from a Ruined City,* according to Fitzpatrick, marked a change in Abdoh's HIV+ work:

> When we started to get the text, finally, after two and a half weeks of mak-
> ing the framework, he came back to rehearsal [after a bout with pneumonia]
> looking very spectral and ill indeed, and was so pleased at how the company
> had functioned creating the framework, and he could drop the stuff in. We
> got the text and we started to do it fast and loud, á la the old shows, á la *Bo-
> geyman* and *Hip-Hop* and *Law of Remains.* And he said "no, no, not like
> that. I want this to be very slow, painfully slow.""But what about the old
> way, the fast and loud way?"—God, I can never remember quotes—[Abdoh
> said] something like "I think I've gone beyond that now," which was just
> like signaling the end of an era. And we all went "thank God, man!" Cause
> it's hard to do it that fast and that loud.[35]

If *Quotations* subsumed the anger of earlier post-HIV+ productions under an encompassing late-century *theatrum mundi* seen from the decaying center of Western economic, political, and image-making power, this strategy in no way diminished the centrality of AIDS in the work. It did, on the other hand, create a brilliant theatrical response to what Simon Watney has called "The Spectacle of AIDS": the "carefully and elaborately stage-managed [. . .] sensational didactic pageant" performed ubiquitously through Western European and North American mass-media culture and through AIDS "education," in which the diseased bodies of gay men are ritually expunged from a dominant sociopolitical structure bent on reenshrining the patriarchal family as the "national family unit," a "private" model for "public" social organization.[36] The ongoing spectacle of AIDS focuses on the homosexual body as the "source" of disease, disease that specifically "threatens" other physical bodies, but more importantly, metaphorically threatens State, Family, and Society. *Quotations from a Ruined City* is a different sort of spectacle, in which Reza Abdoh presented the same elements in reverse symbological order. In Abdoh's spectacle, State, Family, and Society are centers of critical attention, while the HIV+ body coexists on a more metaphoric level.

Quotations from a Ruined City marks two related shifts in late-twentieth-century performance. Its first shift, from postmodernist political detachment to post-postmodernist political engagement, is made possible by its second shift: a recognition of the "structural stability" of avant-garde theater techniques since their inception in the 1890s. Working within the theatricality of those techniques, Abdoh also moved beyond postmodernist performance's reliance on irony as a dominating sensibility. *Quotations from a Ruined City* returns not only to an engagement with issues characteristic of other political theaters of this century, but also to the ritual focus on death, birth, and renewal that characterizes Ta'ziyeh and other folk theaters. Finally, Abdoh even recovered romance, in *Quotations'* penultimate image of the two lovers embracing on the floor. They are most certainly doomed; the hanging sides of meat which are the production's ultimate image underline that fact. Nonetheless, in an artful quotation from Hollywood-style sensibilities, Abdoh here indulged in hope, not necessarily on the grand scale of political and social renewal, about which Abdoh was too realistically skeptical, but on the smaller, more important scale of personal relations, which hinge on the possibility of love.

Notes

1. My use of the term "postmodernist theater" in this essay avoids dealing with the different strategies of feminist and queer performance which, although often sharing performance techniques with high postmodernist theater, cannot as easily afford disconnected neutrality. For queer and feminist theater, the mere existence of the performance takes on inevitable political overtones, whether or not those are taken up as thematic subjects.

2. L. C. Cole, "Angrier Than Thou," in *New York Native,* March 14, 1994, p. 33.

3. Robert Sember, personal communication with author, September 21, 1994.

4. Reza Abdoh, interview with author, April 5, 1994.

5. Reza Abdoh and Salar Abdoh, *Quotations from a Ruined City, TDR* 39, no. 4 (T148) (Fall 1995): 114–15.

6. Exceptions were an exhibition by émigré Bosnian artists, a symposium on Bosnia by New York artists and activists, and the Bread and Puppet Theater's *Fly or Die,* based on the testimonies of Bosnian rape vicitims.

7. Abdoh and Abdoh, p. 110.

8. A further example of this complexity is the "Impalement" text itself. Abdoh insisted that he found the text in a French journal (interview with author, April 5, 1994), and at first hearing it sounds like the first-person testimony of a contemporary refugee. (First-person testimonies by Bosnian women raped by Serbian men were highly publicized at this time.) But as Lenio Myrivili has pointed out to me, the impalement story is in fact based on Ivo Andric's acclaimed 1945 novel of Yugoslavian history, *Na Drini Cuprija* (*The Bridge on the Drina*) (trans. Lovett F. Edwards [New York: Macmillan], 1959). Andric, a Bosnian Serb, set the impalement scene in the sixteenth century, as an example of the cruelties of the Turkish occupation of Bosnia (pp. 48–51). In Andric's version, the Muslim Turks impale a rebellious Serbian peasant. Abdoh's version reverses sides and sets the story in the present.

9. Abdoh and Abdoh, pp. 135–36.

10. Michael C. Hillman, *Unity in the Ghazels of Hafiz* (Minneapolis: Bibliotheca Islamica, 1976), p. 2.

11. Reza Abdoh, interview with author, April 5, 1994.

12. Peter Avery and John Heath-Stubbs, *Hafiz of Shiraz* (London: John Murray, 1952), pp. 8–9.

13. Henri Broms, *Two Studies in the Relation of Hafiz and the West* (Helsinki: Societas Orientalis Fennica, 1968), p. 8.

14. See William O. Beeman, *Cultural Performance of Communication in Iran* (Tokyo: Institute for the Study of Languages and Cultures of Asia and Africa, 1982); Peter Chelkowski, ed., *Ta'ziyeh: Ritual and Drama in Iran* (New York: New York University Press, 1979); and Milla Riggio, ed., *Ta'ziyeh: Ritual and Popular Beliefs in Iran* (Hartford, Conn.: Trinity College, 1988).

15. Beeman, p. 121. According to Beeman's analysis of Ta'ziyeh, "'literal time' . . . [is] the actual time it takes for dialogue to take place from beginning to end"; "'representational time is truncated, elongated or distorted time" (i.e., battle scenes which take less time than in real life); and "'non-time' is a kind of dimension which allows the co-occurrence of all sorts of characters and events which could not possibly have existed together at the same time." Similarly, Beeman notes, "'literal space' surrounds most encounters between characters, and events"; "'representational space' compresses or elongates actual space" in travel or battlefield scenes; and "'non-space' creates the co-occurrence of personages far removed from each other spatially as well as temporally" (p. 121).

16. Andréa R. Vaucher, *Muses from Chaos and Ash: AIDS, Artists, and Art* (New York: Grove Press, 1993), p. 45.

17. Reza Abdoh, interview with author, February 18, 1994.

18. Hal Foster, "For a Concept of the Political in Contemporary Art," in *Recordings: Art, Spectacle, Cultural Politics* (Port Townsend, Wash.: Bay Press, 1985), p. 155.

19. Roland Barthes, "The Death of the Author," in *Image-Music-Text* (New York: Hill and Wang, 1977), p. 147.

20. Philip Auslander, "Toward a Concept of the Political in Postmodern Theatre," *Theatre Journal* 39, I (March 1987): 21.

21. John Bell, "*Roy Cohn / Jack Smith*," *Theater Week,* March 9, 1992, pp. 12–13.

22. This connection was uncannily underlined in the New York production of *Quotations* by the presence of longtime Living Theatre actor Tom Walker as the Arab Man.

23. Jochen Schülte-Sasse, "Theory of Modernism versus Theory," in Foreword to *Theory of the Avant-Garde,* by Peter Bürger, trans. by Michael Shaw (Minneapolis: University of Minnesota Press, 1984), p. xxxvii.

24. Peter Bürger, *Theory of the Avant-Garde,* trans. by Michael Shaw (Minneapolis: University of Minnesota Press, 1984), p. 18.

25. Ibid., p. 56.

26. Walter Benjamin, *The Origin of German Tragic Drama,* trans. by John Osborne (London: Verso, 1977), p. 178.

27. Frantisek Déak, "Structuralism in Theatre: The Prague School Contribution," *TDR* 20, no. 4 (T72) (Fall 1976): 90.

28. Reza Abdoh, interview with the author, February 18, 1994.

29. Jindrich Honzl, "Dynamics of the Sign in the Theater," in *Semiotics of Art,* ed. by Ladislav Matejka and Irwin R. Titunik (Cambridge: MIT Press, 1986), p. 79.

30. Ibid., p. 80.

31. Timothy Wiles, *The Masks of Menander: Sign and Meaning in Greek and Roman Performance* (New York: Cambridge University Press, 1991), p. 13.

32. Reza Abdoh, interview with the author, April 5, 1994.

33. Abdoh and Abdoh, p. 127.

34. Tom Fitzpatrick, interview with the author, March 30, 1994.

35. Ibid.

36. Simon Watney, "The Spectacle of AIDS," in *The Lesbian and Gay Studies Reader,* ed. by Henry Abelove, Michèle Aina Barale, and David M. Halperin (New York: Routledge, 1993), p. 209.

Additional Sources Consulted

Brantley, Ben. "*Quotations* from a Ruined City." *New York Times,* March, 3 1994, p. C20.

Fuchs, Elinor. "A Vision of Ruin." *Village Voice,* March 15, 1994, pp. 91–92.

Leverett, James. "Ghosts of Obies Past." *Village Voice,* May 31, 1994, p. 100.

Savran, David. *The Wooster Group, 1975–1985: Breaking the Rules.* Ann Arbor, Mich.: UMI Research Press, 1986.

Stayton, Richard. "Hellraiser: The Shock Tactics of Reza Abdoh Push Audiences to the Edge." *American Theatre* 8, no. 11 (February 1992): 26–33.

Elinor Fuchs

Always Staging *Lear*

After a performance of *Tight Right White,* the third of Reza Abdoh's four pieces produced in New York, I had a brief conversation with Reza and his producer, Diane White, who were standing at the entrance to the playing space in the cavernous industrial loft. "That last scene was absolutely out of *King Lear,*" I commented. "Well yes," said Reza to my surprise, "that's what it was supposed to be." Subsequently I learned that in Los Angeles, at the age of 21, Reza had directed his own adaptation of *King Lear,* a four-and-a-half-hour production performed in a small Hollywood performance space above a store that seated, according to White's memory, about forty spectators a night. The night White saw it, Reza himself stood in for a missing actor and played Edgar.

In the course of following Reza's work in New York (I did not see the earlier work created in Los Angeles performed live, though I have seen some of it on videotape) I came to think that *Lear,* in its relentless probing of the extremes of cruelty, psychological disintegration, and physical vulnerability, was a constant template for his imagination. More specifically, Reza created "heath scenes." The "heath" in Abdoh, however, was not a scene of howling winds and raging storm. Rather, these scenes were uncharacteristically still and silent. They took place, perhaps, in the silent eye of the storm. As in *Lear,* they were always marked by a direct relation to nature, a setting otherwise almost antithetical to Abdoh's work. Most important, these were scenes of metaphysical exposure to the buffets of existence, where characters were stripped to a common human identity, the "bare, forked animal" itself.

In these moments, the masks of cruelty and irony would drop, the hellish boil of human conflict that was Reza's subject would subside, and the stage figures would be revealed *sub specie aeternitatis,* suddenly frail. They were reduced to gasping for breath, as in *Tight Right White,* or crawling towards each other over the bone yard of human culture in *Quotations from a Ruined City.*

The Law of Remains intertwined the sadism of Jeffrey Dahmer and the vacant exhibitionism of Andy Warhol in what may have been Abdoh's most savage performance. It was performed in the decrepit Diplomat Hotel, now demolished, on West 43rd Street. There were video scenes of flesh-peeling autopsies, tormented characters in wire cages, assaultive chorus lines whisking down to the genitals in repeated deadpan strip dances, and an "electrocution" of Dahmer accompanied by plates of bones shoved in the faces of resisting spectators, then shattered on the floor—all played against an ear-splitting musical and verbal cacophony. The lights went to black, then silence. When they came up, the spectators were requested to file out of the performance space.

At the back of the hall was a hitherto unnoticed setting: a grove of dead trees. The entire cast stood in motionless pairs among these trees, stripped naked, silent, and intently returning our gaze. It was gaze for gaze. The only sound was the tolling of bells—a knell, for them? for us? Here was a version of the heath. A moment ago these figures were armored with an entire repertoire of threatening sounds and gestures. Now, but for their boots—they still have boots—they have taken inadequate refuge in an unsheltering nature, wordless, and stripped to essential skin.

The scene on the heath marks the central turning point in the action of *King Lear.* After the heath, Lear is in flight to Dover; Gloucester's eyes are put out, and he too struggles towards Dover; Edgar begins his slow return from Bedlam; Cordelia's forces start to turn the tide. But for Abdoh, it was as if the play was over once he had reached the essential revelation: compassion was owed to all "poor naked wretches" whose "houseless heads and unfed sides" endure the storm.

After the dead forest of *The Law of Remains,* the performance continued for one more scene in the ruined upper ballroom of the Hotel Diplomat. But this coda took place in a kind of diabolic "heaven," the figures were now shrouded in white and clearly in an enactment that took place after death. Death was the only scene that could follow Abdoh's heaths.

Tight Right White was Abdoh's scream of protest against racism and homophobia in historical and present-day America. Played, danced, sung, mimed, and masked with frantic energy among ten stage areas, and interspersed with clips and reenacted scenes from the film *Man-*

dingo, the elements of the piece were connected through the recurring figures of a young black (ironically played by a white man in blackface) and a loud, vulgar turn-of-the-century Jewish vaudeville figure, Moishe Pipik. Both search for a "real" identity amid the forces that would make the search impossible: the slave plantation, the KKK, Nazis old and neo-, withering racial humor. Meanwhile Little Eliza crosses the ice; a Jew sings a love song in Auschwitz.

It was the final scene that made a direct allusion to the heath scene in *Lear.* The spectators, who had followed the actors from stage to stage, returned to their first positions on the floor, facing the ramp that connected two large, square stages to right and left. On the right (the directional symbolism perhaps not unintended) was a silent family camping scene, a kind of "scout" scene with white tent, white clothing, plump white children, white marshmallows, the white of purity and privilege. The figures in this scene were half-hidden behind their tent and absorbed in adjusting their equipment. They could not see the wrenching scene on the opposite stage. Across the way, in the contrasting white of a silent snowfall, stood a line of trembling half-naked wretches, gripping their exaggeratedly racial, and now pathetic, carnival masks. The shivering was the reference to "Poor Tom's a-cold" of the heath that I took Abdoh to acknowledge in our conversation.

As in the heath scene of *King Lear,* these matching scenes in *Tight Right White* depended on the audience's understanding of the subjection of the figures to "pitiless" nature. The figures on the left might not survive; the figures on the right doubled nature's indifference: they couldn't care less.

In the foreground on the left stage sat Blaster, the young "black" man, hooked to yet another mask, an oxygen mask. The only sound in the otherwise silent scene was his racked coughing and gasping for breath. Symphonic music builds ("The Damnation of Faust"?), over which could be heard the faint repeated whisper, "Who will be the witness?" There would be no witnesses, was my reading; no one from this chorus line of color and poverty would be left to mourn, no matter what color their mask. These holy fools of the piece would share the fate of Lear's Fool, who vanished from the scene without a trace.

In Reza's final piece, *Quotations from a Ruined City,* the heath scene no longer stood in isolated contrast to an otherwise feverish performance. Here it spread out to become a series of recurring scenes that linked the piece together. It was as if the space of natural and metaphysical exposure symbolized by the heath now contained all strands of figure and incident.

It is not surprising that the final destination of the idea of heath, as I take Reza to have been using it, should have been the cemetery. It was a short move from the dead forest of *Law of Remains,* to the frigid snowfall of *Tight Right White,* to the site of death itself. At one level, of course, this recurring scene was the artist's announcement of his own impending death. But at the geopolitical level that so urgently ran through this piece, the cemetery, like Lear's heath, became the great leveler of human difference. Its traditional symbolism collapsed the explosive cultural differences within Los Angeles, Sarajevo, and Beirut, the deadly Bermuda Triangle of "ruined cities" the piece evoked.

The dark and silent opening of *Quotations* appeared to be a landscape scattered with driftwood. As the lights warmed, the organic driftwood forms were revealed to be bandage-wrapped human figures. Then the gravestones behind them appeared: the landscape had merged into the cemetery. The scene soon shifted to the narrative Abdoh wove that ranged from the historic violence of American capitalism to the contemporary violence of ethnic hatreds. But the cemetery scene recurred, each time in a different guise, always beneath the sky of nature. At one point, not without an ironic wink, it reappeared backed by a flock of cardboard sheep and the twitter of birdsong. Here was a curious development: after the forbidding metaphorical cemeteries of the previous pieces—the dead forest, the freezing snowfall—a certain lightness of spirit becomes possible in the graveyard itself.

"I have been obsessed with doing Lear and have even dreamed about it," Abdoh told a *Los Angeles Times* interviewer in January 1985. "The structure of the play is one of the most magnificent achievements man has ever done. It's right there with Dante's *Inferno* and Wagner's *Parsifal.*" The comparisons suggest that Reza thought of *King Lear* as a kind of Passion play, and ultimately as a play of redemption. "Everybody thinks of [*Lear*] in terms of darkness and dreariness," he told the interviewer, apparently aware that his regenerative view of the play had fallen out of critical favor, "but I see the flight of Lear's and Cordelia's souls as . . . uplifting and purified."

The Passion play, making plays of suffering and redemption, was what Reza's New York work was increasingly about. His first production in New York, *Father Was a Peculiar Man,* a loose adaptation of *The Brothers Karamazov* staged in the streets of the wholesale meat district of Manhattan, became directly that in the near-final scene. A green Christ was crucified just below a shop sign implacably announcing the slaughter of the innocents, "Fresh Killed Baby Spring Lamb." An echo of this moment appeared at the end of *Quotations,* when enormous cutouts of butchered beef, lowered from the ceiling on meat hooks, provided a backdrop to the final moments of dying lovers crawling towards each other across the stage.

Reza Abdoh's work was in the broadest sense permanently located on the heath: it was situated on the ground where there is no protection from the storm, life as storm. Around the wretches gathered there he then proceeded to create a theater of fierce protectiveness, with an impulse to value every human soul, down to the most vile. He unrolled a dazzling horror show, but even the evil actors on the universal scene were victims of illusion and quivering with fear. Everyone was a side of beef and a lamb of God in his work. He never tried to solve that "problem." One of the appeals of *King Lear* may have been its immense consciousness of human contradiction. It is sharply confronted in the heath scene, as Lear rips off his garments to join Edgar's "unaccommodated man."

Abdoh's sense of the range of human experience went to places our theater cannot for the most part even imagine. Robert Wilson has always said that *King Lear* was better in the mind's eye than on the stage, which could only reduce its size, but Reza's theater uttered screams of rage, compassion, and truth of *Lear*-like dimensions. His was truly theater at the limit.

Chronology

1963   23 February, born in Iran.

1970   Sees Peter Brooks's production of *A Midsummer Night's Dream* in London.

1972-82 Editor's note: Reza Abdoh's brother, Salar, has informed me that previously published biographical information about Reza's activities during this period was incorrect. It appears that Reza Abdoh, when he began his career, may have embellished parts of his curriculum vitae pertaining to the years from 1972 until 1982. Salar and Reza's mother, Homa Oboodi, informed me, for example, that Reza never performed in the Robert Wilson production "KA MOUNTAIN, GUARDenia TERRACE." It is difficult to prove beyond doubt that someone did not do something he claimed to have done, particularly if one is talking about having directed a play at a small theater more than fifteen years ago, but much of the previously published information about Abdoh's pre-adult life appears suspect. At the time of publication, the National Youth Theatre was being renovated and could not retrieve the records I requested; it is not clear if Abdoh ever studied there, or what his activities there may have been. Salar Abdoh maintains that *Peer Gynt,* Reza's first directorial project, was staged not at the National Youth Theatre, as has been maintained in numerous publications, but at the Wellington Boarding School in Somerset, where the two brothers were enrolled. Reza Abdoh claimed to have traveled to India to study Kathakali in 1979, but Salar says that Reza never went to India. The University of Southern California's Records Office informed me that he matriculated only for one semester, in the fall of 1979. In 1979 he aslo published a book of poetry never mentioned in subsequent articles or interviews: *The Sound of a Poet Breathing in An Imprisoned Air.* Finally, perhaps as a result of anti-Iranian sentiment at about the time he arrived in Los

Angeles, Reza informed people that his mother was Italian. She is Iranian.

1983   Directs *Three Plays by Howard Brenton* (*Pristine Love, Heads,* and *Saliva Milkshake*) at Fifth Estate Theater, Los Angeles.

Serves as assistant director for *One-Acts,* by Samuel Beckett, directed by Alan Mandell, at Los Angeles Theatre Center, Los Angeles.

1984   Directs *King Lear* at Gangway Performance Center, Los Angeles.

1985   Directs *The Farmyard,* by Franz Xaver Kroetz, at Theater Upstairs, Los Angeles.

Directs *The Sound of a Voice* and *As the Crow Flies,* by David Henry Hwang, at Los Angeles Theatre Center, Los Angeles.

1986   Adapts, from Euripides, and directs *A Medea: Requiem for a Boy with a White White Toy* at Hollywood Gymnasium, Los Angeles.

Writes *Rusty Sat on a Hill One Dawn and Watched the Moon Go Down* and directs it at Stages Theater, Los Angeles.

Creates videos *My Face* and *Oh Thello Sit Still.*

1987   Adapts, from Sophocles, and directs *King Oedipus* at Theater Upstairs, Los Angeles.

Directs *Eva Peron,* by Copí, at Theater Upstairs, Los Angeles.

Creates videos *Jane Kirkpatrick in My Bathtub* and *Tiger Turd.*

1988   Directs *Peep Show,* by Abdoh and Mira-Lani Oglesby, at Hollywood Highland Hotel, Los Angeles; wins *L.A. Weekly*'s Production of the Year Award.

Creates videos *Demon Lover* and *Loose Ends.*

1989   Directs *Minamata,* by Abdoh and Mira-Lani Oglesby, at Los Angeles Theatre Center, Los Angeles.

Creates video *The Boardroom Incident.*

Wins Princess Grace Foundation's U.S.A. Theater Fellowship Award for 1989-90.

1990   Directs *Father Was a Peculiar Man,* by Abdoh and Mira-Lani Oglesby, in the meatpacking district, En Garde Arts, New York.

Writes and directs *The Hip-Hop Waltz of Eurydice* at Los Angeles Theatre Center, Los Angeles.

Directs *Pasos en la Obscuridad,* by Frank Ambriz and Abdoh, at Los Angeles Festival, Los Angeles.

Creates videos *Day of Wrath* and *Sleeping with the Devil.*

1991   *The Hip-Hop Waltz of Eurydice* performed at Festival de Théâtre des Amériques, Montréal.

Writes and directs *Bogeyman* at Los Angeles Theatre Center, Los Angeles.

Creates Dar A Luz theater company.

Wins Los Angeles Cultural Affairs Commission Grant for Film-Making; also the Audrey Skirball-Kenis Theatre Award for Outstanding New Work.

Creates videos *The Weeping Song* and *Daddy's Girl.*

1992   Writes and directs *The Law of Remains*, performed by Dar A Luz, at Diplomat Hotel, New York City.

Tours *The Law of Remains* to Walker Art Center, Minneapolis.

Directs *Simon Boccanegra*, by Giuseppe Verdi, at Long Beach Opera, Long Beach, California.

The Hip-Hop Waltz of Eurydice performed at Sigma Festival, Bordeaux, and Mercat des la Flors, Barcelona.

Writes and directs *The Blind Owl* (90-minute feature film).

1993   Writes and directs *Tight Right White*, performed by Dar A Luz, at 440 Lafayette Street, New York City.

Tours *The Law of Remains* to Springdome Festival, Utrecht; Festival Internacional, Granada; Wiener Festwochen, Vienna; Internationales Tanzfestival, Munich; Theater am Turm, Frankfurt-am-Main; Sommertheater, Hamburg, from May until July.

Stages workshop performance of *Quotations from a Ruined City* at Los Angeles Festival in August.

Tours *The Hip-Hop Waltz of Eurydice* and *The Law of Remains* to Fesitval d'Automne, Paris, in November.

1994   Directs *Quotations from a Ruined City*, by Reza Abdoh and Salar Abdoh, performed by Dar A Luz, at 448 West 16th Street, New York City.

1995   May 5, is among the first five winners of the CalArts/Alpert Award in the Arts.

Dies in New York City on May 11.

1996   Posthumously receives a "Bessie" Choreographer and Creator Award for Sustained Achievement.

Select Bibliography

One book of poetry by Reza Abdoh is known to have been published:

The Sound of a Poet Breathing in An Imprisoned Air. New York: Vantage Press, 1979.

Published and Unpublished Scripts

Several unpublished scripts will be added to the archive at the New York Public Library for the Performing Arts, including *Bogeyman* and *Father Was a Peculiar Man.*

The Law of Remains. In *Plays for the End of the Century*, ed. by Bonnie Marranca. Baltimore: Johns Hopkins University Press, 1996, 9–94.

Quotations from a Ruined City, with Salar Abdoh, in *TDR.* Vol. 39, no. 4 (T148) (Fall 1995): 108–36.

Tight Right White. TheatreForum. No. 4 (Winter/Spring 1994): 63–81.

Videotapes

All of these videotapes are available at the New York Public Library for the Performing Arts at Lincoln Center, the Walker Arts Center in Minneapolis, and at Cal Arts in Valencia, California.

Medea: Requiem for a Boy with a White White Toy. 1986.
Rusty Sat on a Hill One Dawn. 1986.
Video short: *My Face.* 1986.
Video short: *O Thello Sit Still.* (1986).
King Oedipus. 1987.
Eva Peron. 1987.
Video short: *Jean Kirkpatrick in My Bathtub.* 1987.
Video short: *Tiger Turd.* 1987.
Peep Show. 1988
Video short: *Demon Lover.* 1988.

Video short: *Loose Ends*. 1988.
Minamata. 1989.
Video short: *The Boardroom Incident*. 1989.
The Hip-Hop Waltz of Eurydice. 1990.
Pasos en la Obscuridad. 1990.
Video short: *The Day of Wrath*. 1990.
Video short: *Sleeping with the Devil*. 1990.
Bogeyman. 1991.
Video short: *Daddy's Girl*. 1991.
Video short: *The Weeping Song*. 1991.
The Law of Remains. 1992.
Simon Boccanegra. 1992.
Feature-length film: *The Blind Owl*. 1992.
Tight Right White. 1993.
Quotations from a Ruined City. 1994.
Feature-length film: *Train Project*. Unfinished.
Interviews. Various dates.
Memorial Ceremony, Los Angeles. 1995
Memorial Ceremony, New York, 1995.

Interviews with Reza Abdoh

Bell, John. "To Reach Divinity through the Act of Performance." *TDR* 39, no. 4 (T148) (Fall 1995): 48–71.
Bergelt, Martin, and Hortensia Völckers. "Gewalt—Tod—Theater: Ein Gesprach." (Interview with H. Volckers and M. Bergelt). *Akzente-Zeitschrift für Literatur* 40, no. 2 (April 1993): 164–73.
Féral, Josette. "Theatre Is Not about Theory." *TDR* 39, no. 4 (T148) (Fall 1995): 86–96.
Fischer, Eva-Elisabeth. "Ein Gespräch mit dem Theatermann Reza Abdoh." *Süddeutsche Zeitung,* June 2, 1993.
Leabhart, Thomas. "Reza Abdoh." *Mime Journal*, vol. 2 (1991): 11–27. (Leabhart interviewed Abdoh, then omitted his questions, organizing the answers into essay form.)
Lepecki, André. "Fragments de la cité des horreurs." *Mouvement*, no. 8 (July–August 1994): 6–9.
Marquardt, Hans-Werner. "Soll ich jeden Morgen heulen und schreien?" *Berliner Zeitung*, October 11, 1994.
Mufson, Daniel. January 14, 1995, interview in "Places Ripped Open Again and Again: Sex, Identity, and Death in the Recent Works of Reza Abdoh." Unpublished master's thesis, Yale University, 1995.
Vaucher, Andréa R. *Muses from Chaos and Ash: AIDS, Artists, and Art*. New York: Grove Press, 1993.

Wehle, Philippa. "Reza Abdoh and *Tight Right White:* Interviews with Reza Abdoh." *TheatreForum,* no. 4 (Fall/Winter 1994): 57–59.

Articles, Reviews, and Theses on the Artist

Arkatov, Janice. "Everything Goes in Abdoh Plays." *Los Angeles Times,* December 6, 1986, Calendar, 2.

Artel, Sabrina. "At Breakneck Speed." *TDR* 39, no. 4 (Fall 1995): 72–85.

Bell, John. "AIDS and Avant-garde Classicism: Reza Abdoh's *Quotations from a Ruined City.*" *TDR* 39, no. 4 (T148) (Fall 1995): 21–47.

———. "The Law of Remains." *Theater Week,* March 23, 1992.

Benach, Joan-Anton. "Orfeo, Eurídice y el apocalipsis." *La Vanguardia,* November 22, 1992, 62.

Brantley, Ben. "Quotations from a Ruined City" (review). *New York Times,* March 3, 1994, C20.

Bus, Rosemarie. "Ein Mann für jeden Schock." *Cosmopolitan International,* no. 6 (June 1993): 214–18.

Carlson, Marvin. "Back to the Basics" (review of *Tight Right White*). *Journal of Dramatic Theory and Criticism* 8, no. 2 (1993): 187–91.

———. "Father Was a Peculiar Man" (review). *Journal of Dramatic Theory and Criticism* 5, no. 2 (1991): 193–96.

Coleman, Beth. "It's a Family Affair: Reza Abdoh's Theater of Pangs." *Village Voice,* March 16, 1993, 39.

Collins, Glenn. "Street Theater Audience Must Make a Choice." *New York Times,* July 19, 1990, C17.

———. "Theatrical Director's Calling Card: Sex and Death." *New York Times,* February 24, 1992, C1.

Dasgupta, Gautam. "Body/Politic: The Ecstasies of Reza Abdoh." *Performing Arts Journal* 16, no. 3 (September 1994): 19–28.

Drake, Sylvie. "Abdoh Stumbles with 'Pasos.'" *Los Angeles Times,* September 8, 1990, Calendar, 5.

———. "A Chaotic Plaint for Our Fouled Nest." *Los Angeles Times,* May 14, 1989.

———. "Exorcising Demons." *Los Angeles Times,* August 30, 1991, F1.

———. "A Waltz on the Wild Side." *Los Angeles Times,* December 14, 1990.

Feingold, Michael. "Tight Right White" (review). *Village Voice,* March 23, 1993, pp. 93, 97.

Fischer, Eva-Elisabeth. "Vergewaltigung durch Moral." *Ballett international tanz aktuell* (October 1994): 37–38.

Fuchs, Elinor. "The Performance of Mourning." *American Theatre* (January 1993): 14–17.

———. "Play as Landscape: Another Version of Pastoral." *Theater* 25, no. 1 (Spring/Summer 1994): 44–52.

———. "A Vision of Ruin" (review of *Quotations from a Ruined City*). *Village Voice*, March 15, 1994, 91–92.

Godard, Colette. "Les Etats-Unis en images éclatées." *Le Monde*, November 17, 1992, 18.

Goldman, Jeffrey. "An Absurd, Exhausting *Peep Show* Makes Voyeurs of the Audience." *Village View*, April 22–28, 1988, 5.

Holden, Stephen. "A Carnival of Satire and Savagery, with a Karamazov as Ringmaster." *New York Times*, July 11, 1990.

Jacobson, Lynn. "Poison in the Bay." *American Theatre* (June 1989): 6.

King, Kenneth. "Reza Abdoh's *Quotations from a Ruined City*." *Performing Arts Journal* 16, no. 3 (September 1994): 29–38.

Koehler, Robert. "The Blood Flows in Brenton One-Acts." *Los Angeles Times*, June 17, 1983, part 6, p. 10.

———. "'Oedipus,' 'Peron': How Tyrants Die." *Los Angeles Times*, July 22, 1987, part 5, p. 2.

Marowitz, Charles. "Los Angeles in Review: Bogeyman." *TheaterWeek*, October 14, 1991, 34–35.

Mejías-Rentas, Antonio. "Reza Abdoh disfruta sus 'Pisadas' dentro de la cultura latinoamericana." *La Opinion*, September 6, 1990, section 6, p. 1.

Méreuze, Didier. "Reza Abdoh entre Cocteau et Artaud." *La Croix*, December 4, 1993, 16.

Mikulan, Steven. "Exterminating Angel: Reza Abdoh's Theater of Sacrifice." *L.A. Weekly*, November 29–December 5, 1991, 19–28.

Miller, Daryl H. "Dances with Abdoh." *L.A. Daily News*, December 21, 1990, 31.

Mufson, Daniel. "Places Ripped Open Again and Again: Sex, Identity, and Death in the Recent Works of Reza Abdoh." Unpublished master's thesis, Yale University, 1995.

———. "Same Vision, Different Form: Reza Abdoh's *The Blind Owl*." *TFR* 39, no. 4 (T148) (Fall 1995): 97–107.

Munk, Erika. "Meaty Metaphors." *Village Voice*, July 18–24, 1990, 102.

Neff, Renfreu. "Taking It to the Streets." *Contemporanea* (October 1990): 82–85.

O'Mahony, John. "Shocking Père." *Guardian*, December 7, 1993, 4.

———. "Shockwaves from the Avant-Garde Stage." *Guardian*, May 16, 1995, 16.

Pizzati, Carlo. "Che macello quel teatro." *Il Venerdi di Repubblica*, September 1, 1990, 107–13.

Plagens, Peter, with Lynda Wright. "Multiculturalism or Bust, Gang." *Newsweek*, September 24, 1990, 68.

Román, David. "Bogeyman" (review). *Theatre Journal* 44, no. 3 (October 1992): 395–97.

Roter, Sybille. "Höllentheater ohne Absolution." *Musik and Theater*. September 9, 1993, 8–13.

Sadownick, Douglas. "The Big Band 'Bogeyman': Reza Abdoh Takes on the Gay '90s." *Frontiers*, September 27, 1991.

———. "Hell's Angels" (review of *The Hip-Hop Waltz of Eurydice*). *American Theatre* (February 1991): 9–10.

———. "To Hell and Back: Reza Abdoh Mixes Sex and Mythology for a Hip-Hop Journey to the Underworld." *Advocate*, March 12, 1991, 71.

———. "Who Is Bogeyman?" (program notes). LATC production of *Bogeyman*, 1991.

Sagal, Peter. "Waking Nightmares." *TheaterWeek*, January 14, 1991, 24–28.

Simons, Tad. "The Art of the Unspeakable." *Twin Cities Reader*, October 21–27, 1992, 14–16.

Solis, René. "Abdoh Horror Picture Show." *Libération*, December 3, 1993, 31.

Stayton, Richard. "Hellraiser: The Shock Tactics of Reza Abdoh Push Audiences to the Edge." *American Theatre* 8, no. 11 (February 1992): 26.

———. "L.A. Dramatists Unfold New Tableaux: A Glimpse of Potential." *Los Angeles Herald Examiner*, April 22, 1988, 10.

———. " 'A Medea': An Artist Dares to Dream in This Sober World." *Los Angeles Herald Examiner,* July 26, 1986, B8.

———. "Theater on the Edge." *Los Angeles Times*, August 25, 1991, Calendar, 7.

Sullivan, Dan. "Modern Works Find Use for Legendary Images." *Los Angeles Times*, February 19, 1986, Calendar, 1.

———. "Trysting with Art-Theater at a Hollywood Motel." *Los Angeles Times*, April 19, 1988, part 6, p. 1.

Warfield, Polly. " 'As the Crow Flies' and 'Sound of a Voice'." *Drama-Logue*, February 20–26, 1986.

———. "Eva Peron / King Oedipus." *Drama-Logue*, July 16–22, 1987.

———. "The Hip-Hop Waltz of Eurydice." *Drama-Logue*, December 20, 1990–January 2, 1991, 29.

———. "Peep Show." *Drama-Logue*, April 21–27, 1988.

———. "Rusty Sat on a Hill One Dawn . . . " *Drama-Logue*, December 11–17, 1986.

———. "Staging Two Plays in Repertory: Innovative Reza Abdoh." *Drama-Logue*, July 9–15, 1987.

Wehle, Philippa. "Hatred versus Hope" (review of *Tight Right White*) *American Theatre* 10, no.4 (April 1993): 13.

———. "*Tight Right White*: A Poetic Work of Mourning." *TheatreForum*, no. 4 (Fall/Winter 1994): 57–59.

Wolf, Steven. " 'Hound of the Underworld': Reza Abdoh's Plays of Troubling, Chaotic Redemption." *Los Angeles Downtown News*, January 14, 1991, 1.

Credits

Grateful acknowledgment is made for permission to reprint from the following writers and publishers: to John Bell and *TDR/The Drama Review* for "AIDS and Avant-garde Classicism: Reza Abdoh's *Quotations from a Ruined City*" and "To Reach Divinity through the Act of Performance," both © 1995 New York University and the Massachusetts Institute of Technology; to Marvin Carlson and *The Journal of Dramatic Theory and Criticism* for "Back to the Basics," © 1993 *Journal of Dramatic Theory and Criticism;* to Gautam Dasgupta and *PAJ* for "Body/Politic: The Ecstasies of Reza Abdoh," © 1994 *PAJ;* to Sylvie Drake for "A Chaotic Plaint for Our Fouled Nest" and "A Waltz on the Wild Side," © 1989 and 1990 Sylvie Drake; to Michael Feingold and *The Village Voice* for "Artaud You So," © 1993 *Village Voice;* to Josette Féral and *TDR/The Drama Review* for "Theatre Is Not about Theory," © 1995 New York University and the Massachusetts Institute of Technology; to Elinor Fuchs for "Always Staging *Lear*," © 1997 Elinor Fuchs, and to Elinor Fuchs and *The Village Voice* for "A Vision of Ruin," © 1995 *Village Voice;* to Stephen Holden and *The New York Times* for "Theatre in Review: *The Law of Remains*," © 1992 The New York Times Company; to Thomas Leabhart for "Reza Abdoh," © 1991 Thomas Leabhart; to Charles Marowitz and *Theatre Week* for "Los Angeles in Review: *Bogeyman*," © 1991 *Theatre Week;* to Howard Ross Patlis for "Dark Shadows and Light Forces," © 1992 Howard Ross Patlis; to Andréa R. Vaucher for *Muses of Chaos and Ash: AIDS, Artists, and Art,* © 1993 Andréa R. Vaucher; to Hortensia Völkers and Martin Bergelt and *Theater Schrift* for "Violence—Death—Theatre," © 1992 *Theater Schrift;* and to Philippa Wehle for "Reza Abdoh and *Tight Right White*" and "*Tight Right White:* A Poetic Work of Mourning," both © 1994 Philippa Wehle.

The following have graciously given permission to reproduce their photographs: Joss Bachhofer, Paula Court, Jan Deen, R. Kaufman, Rosemary Kaul, Richard Leibfried, and Annie Leibovitz.